BIG BIDNESS

The Hustlas Guide to Government Contracts

Table of Contents

Lesson I *1*
   KNOW THE RULES OF THE GAME 1
   For the Hood 7

Lesson II *11*
   KNOW THE PLUG 11
   For the Hood 17

Lesson III *19*
   GET YA' COOK RIGHT 19
   For the Hood 25
   Sample Value Proposition 27
   Practice Value Proposition 29

Lesson IV *31*
   KNOW THY ENEMY 31
   For the Hood 37
   Sample SWOT Analysis 41
   Practice SWOT Analysis 43

Lesson V *45*
   GET ON PAPI'S CONTACT LIST 45
   For the Hood 51

Lesson VI *53*
   ASSEMBLE YA TEAM 53
   For the Hood 61

Lesson VII *63*

MAKE AN OFFER THEY CAN'T REFUSE	63
For the Hood	77
Sample Technical Proposal	81
Sample Cost Proposal	85
Lesson VIII	*93*
KEEP YA EAR TO THE STREETS	93
For the Hood	101
Lesson IX	*103*
DON'T PSYCH YASELF OUT	103
For the Hood	107
Lesson X	*109*
BUY THE BLACK CARD	109
For the Hood	119
Resources	*121*
Glossary	*125*

Big BIDness *the Hustlas Guide to Government Contracts*

Text © 2024 Malcolm Ali. Artwork/design © 2024 Malcolm Ali All rights reserved.

This publication is provided "as is" for informational and entertainment purposes. The author and publisher make no representations or warranties regarding the accuracy or completeness of the content and disclaim any liability arising from its use. The strategies and examples are illustrative; outcomes may vary.

Requests for permission to reproduce selections should be directed to: Permissions, Malcolm Ali, m.ali@mrpurchaseorder.com.

Edited by: Malcolm Ali
Cover/Interior: Malcolm Ali

Trademarks: Product and company names mentioned herein are the property of their respective owners and are used for identification purposes only.

Atlanta, GA, USA

Forward

Government contracting is a complex and challenging field that can seem daunting to those who are just starting. There are many rules, regulations, and procedures to follow, and the competition can be fierce. However, with the right knowledge and approach, anyone can successfully navigate the world of government contracting and build a successful business.

This book is a comprehensive guide to government contracting, covering everything from understanding the procurement process to submitting a winning proposal. It is designed to be a resource for both new and experienced government contractors, providing valuable insights and practical advice to help you succeed.

Throughout the book, you will find a range of strategies and tips for building a strong team, writing a technical proposal, submitting a cost proposal, and more. You will also learn about the importance of networking, understanding your competition, and building relationships with government agencies.

Whether you are a small business owner or a seasoned entrepreneur, this book is an essential tool for anyone looking to succeed in government contracting. It is my hope that the information and advice contained in these pages will help you navigate the challenges of government contracting and build a successful business that can compete on a national stage.

Remember, no matter how challenging the road may seem, with hard work, determination, and the right strategies, anything is possible. So, read on and start building your success in government contracting.

Twina Feliciano, MBA
Small Business Coach
Operation Hope, Inc

To my children, who turned responsibility into joy and duty into purpose. I grew up on the saying that if a man does not work, he does not eat. Fatherhood taught me the real weight. If a man does not work, his family goes hungry. Serving you has been my highest honor and the engine behind my mission to help other providers create generational wealth.

Lesson I

KNOW THE RULES OF THE GAME
(Know the rules and regulations of the Government Procurement Process)

The procurement process for city and local government contracts may differ from the federal procurement process, and it's important to understand the rules and regulations that govern the process to win a contract.

The first step is to become familiar with the procurement regulations and requirements specific to the city or local government agency you are pursuing. This may involve researching the agency's procurement policies and procedures, as well as any local ordinances or regulations that may apply.

When pursuing city or local government contracts, it's important to understand that procurement regulations aren't the only requirements you need to meet. Different agencies may have additional requirements that contractors must fulfill to be considered for a contract. One example of such a requirement is having a business license. Many cities and local agencies require contractors to have a business license to operate within their jurisdiction. The process for obtaining a business license varies depending on the location, so it's important to research the specific requirements of the agency you are pursuing.

Another common requirement is registration with the city or local agency. This registration may be required for certain types of contracts or all contractors working with the agency. The registration process usually involves providing basic information about your business, such as your name, address, and contact information.

In addition to these requirements, there may be other regulations or certifications that apply to specific industries or types of contracts. For example, contractors working on construction projects may need to be certified by a specific agency or organization. They may also require specific licensing. For example, an electrician's license will likely be required to bid on any solicitation that requires electrical work.

It's important to research and understand these requirements in advance so that you can prepare accordingly. Failing to meet these requirements can result in disqualification from consideration for a contract, even if your proposal is otherwise strong. Keep in mind that many contracts run for several years, so if you do not meet the requirements, it may be several years before the solicitation is published again.

It is also important to understand the differences between local and federal procurement when pursuing government contracts. While both types of procurement involve the government purchasing goods and services from private businesses, there are several key differences to consider.

One of the main differences is the size and scope of the contracts. Federal procurement typically involves larger contracts that span multiple states or even countries. These contracts are often highly competitive and require a significant number of resources to pursue. On the other hand, local procurement tends to involve smaller contracts that are more localized and may be less competitive.

Another difference is the procurement process itself. Federal procurement is subject to a complex set of regulations and requirements, such as the Federal Acquisition Regulation (FAR). This framework governs every aspect of the procurement process, from soliciting bids to awarding contracts. Local procurement is often less regulated, with each city or agency having its own unique set of regulations and requirements.

The bidding and evaluation process also differs between local and federal procurement. Federal contracts often require a lengthy and detailed proposal that includes technical specifications, pricing, and other requirements. Local contracts may have a simpler bidding process, with fewer requirements for proposals.

One advantage of pursuing local government contracts is that they may not require as much experience or expertise as federal contracts. While federal contracts often require extensive experience and a proven track record of success, local agencies may be more willing to work with contractors who are just starting or who have less experience.

This is because local agencies often prioritize supporting small businesses and promoting economic development within their communities. They may be willing to take a chance on a contractor who has a strong proposal and is eager to learn and grow their business.

However, it's important to note that while local agencies may be more flexible in their requirements, they still have high standards for quality and performance. Contractors should be prepared to demonstrate their ability to meet these standards through their proposals and previous work experience.

Another advantage of pursuing local government contracts is that they may offer more opportunities for networking and building relationships with government officials and other contractors. Local agencies often hold events and meetings for contractors to learn about upcoming opportunities and connect with other businesses in their industry.

To summarize; local government contracts may offer opportunities for businesses with less experience or expertise to break into the government contracting market. However, contractors should still be prepared to demonstrate their ability to meet high standards for quality and performance. Additionally, pursuing local government contracts can offer networking opportunities and help businesses build relationships with governments and other contractors.

Although building these relationships is important, tread carefully as it relates to bidding. Companies have been accused of collusion and can be barred from bidding on future contracts in both the local and federal realms. Collusion is a form of illegal cooperation or conspiracy between two or more companies to defraud or deceive a third party, such as a government agency, by manipulating the competitive bidding process for government contracts.

In the context of government contracting, collusion can occur when two or more companies agree to submit bids that are higher than the fair market value or divide the contracts among themselves without competing fairly with other bidders. Companies can be accused of collusion if they engage in any activity that compromises the fairness and competitiveness of the procurement process. This can include exchanging information about bids, coordinating prices or terms of bids, agreeing not to compete, or submitting false or misleading information in their bids.

Accusations of collusion can lead to serious consequences for the companies involved. They include criminal charges, fines, and suspension or debarment from government contracting. Additionally, it can damage the reputation of the companies and make it more difficult for them to secure future contracts.

It is important for companies to understand and comply with the laws and regulations governing government contracting and to avoid any behavior that could be perceived as collusive or anti-competitive. Companies should compete fairly and transparently for government contracts and avoid any interactions or agreements with other bidders that could be interpreted as collusion.

Adhering to local laws works in your favor as well. You can also hold other companies and the government agency to the same standard by way of challenges. If a contractor believes that a government contract was awarded unfairly or incorrectly, they may have the option to challenge the award. Challenging a contract award can be a complex and time-consuming process, but it can also be an important step to ensure fairness and protect the interests of the contractor.

The process for challenging a contract award varies depending on the agency and the type of contract, but in general, it involves filing a protest or appeal with the appropriate agency or court. The protest or appeal must typically be filed within a specific timeframe, which is often a matter of days or weeks after the contract award is announced.

To successfully challenge a contract award, the contractor must provide evidence that demonstrates that the award was made in violation of applicable laws or regulations, or that the selection process was flawed or biased. This evidence can include documentation of errors or omissions in the procurement process, evidence of bias or conflict of interest among the decision-makers, or evidence that the awardee did not meet the requirements outlined in the solicitation.

Challenging a contract award can be a difficult process, and it may not always result in a favorable outcome for the protesting contractor. However, it can be an important tool for ensuring fairness and transparency in the government contracting process, and for protecting the interests of the contractor and other potential bidders.

For the Hood

Yo, listen up! If you're tryna get in on the government procurement game in your city, you gotta know the rules, baby! It ain't like the streets, you can't just do whatever you want and expect to come out on top. But don't worry, I got you covered. Here's what you need to know about knowing the rules of local government procurement.

First things first, you gotta do your research, homie. Every city has its own set of rules and regulations when it comes to procurement, and you gotta know what they are if you wanna play the game. This means reading up on the city's procurement code, as well as any other laws or regulations that might apply to the specific type of contract you're going for.

Next up, you gotta know who's in charge, ya dig? Every city has a procurement department or office that's responsible for overseeing the procurement process. These folks are the gatekeepers, and if you wanna get in, you gotta know who they are and what they're looking for. Check out the city's website or give 'em a call to find out who you need to talk to.

Once you know the rules and the players, it's time to start preparing your bid. This is where things can get tricky, but if you're smart about it, you can come out on top. One important thing to keep in mind is that many cities have programs and initiatives aimed at promoting opportunities for small businesses to compete for contracts. So, if you're a small biz owner, be sure to look into these programs and see if you qualify. They could give you a leg up in the procurement process.

Another thing to keep in mind is that many cities have specific requirements that you'll need to meet to be eligible for a contract. This could include things like having a business license, being registered with the city, or having certain certifications or qualifications. Make sure you understand these requirements and have everything in order before you submit your bid. The last thing you want is to be disqualified over a technicality.

And finally, remember that the procurement process can be a long and complicated journey. But don't get discouraged, fam. Keep your eyes on the prize and stay focused on your goals. If you put in the work and follow the rules, you just might make a come-up.

In conclusion, knowing the rules of local government procurement is key to winning contracts in the city. Do your research, know who's in charge, and make sure you understand the specific requirements for each contract. With these tips in mind, you'll be well on your way to success in the world of government procurement.

But what the hell is procurement right? I got you! Ayo, check it - you know how when the government needs stuff, they gotta buy it from somebody, right? That's what procurement is all about, my G. It's the process of buying goods and services from outside sources. But it ain't just about buying whatever, whenever. There are a whole lotta rules and regulations that go into it.

See, when the government wants to buy something, they gotta go through a whole process to make sure they're getting the best deal and that everything is on the up and up. They gotta figure out what they need, how much they're willing to pay, and who they're gonna buy it from.

And that's where you come in. If you wanna get in on that government procurement hustle, you gotta know the game. You gotta know the rules, the players, and how to make your bid stand out from the rest.

Now, I ain't gonna front - it can be a tough game to play. But if you do your homework and hustle hard, you can come out on top. And that means getting that government money, ya dig?

So, if you wanna get in on that procurement game, you gotta start by understanding the process. Know what the government is looking for, what the rules are, and how to make your bid the best it can be. And if you can do that, you might just come out on top and get that paper.

Lesson II

KNOW THE PLUG
(Research the Agency You Want to Contract With)

Researching a local government agency is an important part of the procurement process. By understanding the agency's mission, objectives, and requirements, you can position yourself to successfully compete for contracts.

The first step in researching a local government agency is to visit their website. Most agencies have information on their website about their procurement process, upcoming bids, and the types of goods and services they require. You can also find information about the agency's mission, history, and leadership team.

Another way to research a local government agency is to attend meetings and events. Many agencies hold regular meetings and events that are open to the public. By attending these events, you can learn more about the agency's priorities, challenges, and opportunities.

You should also reach out to the agency's procurement staff to learn more about their procurement process. You can ask questions about their requirements, the bidding process, and any upcoming bids. This can help you to better understand how to position your business to successfully compete for contracts.

It's important to research the agency's past contracts and vendors. This can give you insight into the types of contracts the agency typically awards and the vendors they work with. You can use this information to develop a competitive bid that meets the agency's needs and requirements.

Researching past contracts is an essential part of the procurement process for businesses looking to win contracts with local government agencies. By studying past contracts and the vendors that won them, businesses can gain important insights into the types of contracts that the agency typically awards and the specific requirements they look for in a vendor.

Studying past contracts can also help businesses to identify any trends or patterns in the agency's procurement process. For example, if a certain vendor consistently wins contracts in a particular category, it may indicate that the agency has a preference for that vendor or that type of product or service. This information can help businesses to tailor their bids to better match the agency's needs and preferences.

Addressing vendor preference is a crucial aspect of winning government contracts. While government agencies are required to conduct fair and open competitions for contracts, it's not uncommon for agencies to have a history of working with certain vendors or to have a preference for certain types of vendors.

One way to address vendor preference is to do your research and understand the agency's past procurement history. By studying past contracts and the vendors that won them, you can identify any patterns or preferences that the agency may have. This information can help you tailor your bid to better align with the agency's needs and preferences.

Another strategy is to build relationships with agency personnel and decision-makers. While it's important to avoid any appearance of impropriety or favoritism, building rapport with agency officials can help you gain a better understanding of their needs and priorities. Additionally, by establishing yourself as a reliable and trustworthy vendor, you can increase your chances of winning future contracts.

It's also important to focus on your strengths and capabilities when bidding on government contracts. By highlighting your unique expertise and experience, you can differentiate yourself from other vendors and demonstrate your value to the agency.

Submitting an Open Records Request can be an effective way to learn more about a government agency you are interested in contracting with. An Open Records Request is a request for access to public records, which are documents or information that are made available to the public by law.

Before submitting an Open Records Request, it's important to identify the specific agency or department you are interested in and the type of information you are seeking. This can help ensure that your request is targeted and focused and increases your chances of obtaining the information you need.

To submit an Open Records Request, you will need to follow the procedures established by the agency or jurisdiction in question. This may involve completing a specific form or submitting a written request that outlines the specific information you are seeking.

It's important to note that Open Records Requests can take time to process, and the agency may charge a fee for copying and processing documents. However, the information obtained through an Open Records Request can be invaluable in helping you understand the inner workings of the agency, including its policies, procedures, and past performance.

Requesting copies of proposals through Open Records can provide valuable insight and give companies a competitive advantage in the bidding process. By obtaining copies of successful proposals from previous contracts, companies can analyze the strategies and techniques used by successful bidders to win contracts.

Through analysis of successful proposals, companies can gain a better understanding of what the government agency values and prioritizes in their decision-making process. This can include elements such as technical expertise, past performance, pricing strategies, and compliance with regulations.

Studying successful proposals can also help companies identify gaps in their proposals and make necessary improvements. By learning from the strengths and weaknesses of previous proposals, companies can tailor their proposals to be more competitive and increase their chances of success in future bids.

Generating a library of successful bid proposals from other companies can provide several advantages in the government contracting process. Firstly, by studying successful proposals, companies can gain a better understanding of the government agency's priorities and preferences when it comes to evaluating proposals. This knowledge can inform a company's proposal development process, allowing them to tailor their proposal to the specific needs of the government agency and increase their chances of success.

Secondly, a library of successful bid proposals can serve as a valuable resource for companies seeking to improve their proposal writing skills. By analyzing the format, structure, and language of successful proposals, companies can learn how to better communicate their value proposition and differentiate themselves from their competitors.

Thirdly, having a library of successful proposals can provide a competitive advantage when bidding on contracts. By leveraging the insights gained from studying successful proposals, companies can develop stronger proposals that are better positioned to win contracts.

Finally, having access to a library of successful proposals can save time and resources in the proposal development process. Rather than starting from scratch every time a company submits a proposal, it can draw on the best practices and successful strategies of others, streamlining its proposal development process.

In conclusion, researching the government agency that you want to contract with and building a library of successful bid proposals can greatly benefit companies in the government contracting process. By understanding the specific regulations, requirements, and preferences of the government agency, companies can tailor their proposals and increase their chances of success.

Additionally, by studying successful proposals from other companies, they can gain insights into best practices and strategies that can inform their proposal development process, ultimately leading to more competitive and successful proposals. These practices can save time, and resources, and increase a company's ability to win government contracts. In summary, researching and studying successful bid proposals are critical steps in the government contracting process and can provide a significant competitive advantage for companies seeking to do business with the government.

For the Hood

Yo, listen up! If you're trying to get into the game of government contracting, you gotta do your homework. That means researching the agency you wanna contract with, so you know what they're looking for. It's like studying the game, just like Nas studied the greats to become one of the best rappers of all time.

And once you've done your research, it's time to build up your skills. One way to do that is by building a library of successful bid proposals from other companies. It's like studying Nas's flow, or Biggie's wordplay, to get inspiration for your rhymes. You gotta learn from the best to be the best.

But don't get it twisted, building a library of successful bid proposals ain't about copying someone else's style. It's about learning from their techniques, their strategies, and their mistakes. You gotta take what works for them and make it work for you.

Yo, I know it might sound like we're tryna bite someone else's flow when we talkin' 'bout building a library of successful bid proposals, but it's all about taking notes from the greats in the game, you feel me? It's like how Nas studied the greats before him to learn from their techniques, their strategies, and their mistakes.

You gotta do the same thing when it comes to the government contract game. You gotta take what works for others and make it work for you. It's all about knowing the rules of the game and using that knowledge to your advantage. You don't wanna be out here reinventing the wheel when you can be following a proven formula for success.

Just like Nas didn't become a legend overnight, you won't win a government contract without putting in the work. But if you do your research and build up your skills, you'll be spittin' rhymes (or writing proposals) like a pro in no time. So, get out there and hustle, and remember: to be the best, you gotta learn from the best.

Lesson III

GET YA' COOK RIGHT
(Create a Strong Value Proposition)

When it comes to government contracting, having a strong value proposition can make all the difference. A value proposition is essentially a statement that outlines what your company offers and why it's unique. It's an essential part of your pitch to the government agency you're trying to contract with, as it can help you stand out from the competition and demonstrate why you're the best choice for the job.

So how do you create a strong value proposition? Here are some steps to follow:

Identify Your Unique Selling Points
The first step is to identify what makes your company unique. What sets you apart from other companies in your industry? What are your strengths and key competencies? This could be anything from having a strong track record of delivering projects on time and within budget, to having specialized expertise in a certain area.

Define Your Target Market
Next, it's important to define your target market. Who are you trying to sell to? In the case of government contracting, your target market is the government agency or department that you're trying to contract with.

It's important to research and understand the needs and priorities of your target market so that you can tailor your value proposition accordingly.

Understand Your Customer's Pain Points

Once you've identified your target market, it's important to understand their pain points. What challenges are they facing? What problems are they trying to solve? By understanding your customer's pain points, you can tailor your value proposition to address these specific needs.

Craft Your Value Proposition

Based on your unique selling points, target market, and customer pain points, it's time to craft your value proposition. Your value proposition should be a clear and concise statement that outlines what your company offers and why it's unique. It should highlight the benefits that you can provide to the government agency and explain how you can help them achieve their goals.

Test Your Value Proposition

Once you've crafted your value proposition, it's important to test it out. This can involve getting feedback from colleagues, customers, or other stakeholders, and seeing how they respond to your value proposition. You may need to make some tweaks and adjustments along the way to ensure that your value proposition is as strong and effective as possible.

Overall, creating a strong value proposition is a key component of successful government contracting. By identifying your unique selling points, defining your target market, understanding your customer's pain points, and crafting a compelling value proposition, you can position your company for success and stand out from the competition.

Once you have written your value proposition, it can be helpful to get feedback from an unassociated procurement professional. This person can provide an outside perspective and offer suggestions for improvement. Here are some steps to follow when seeking feedback on your value proposition:

Identify a procurement professional: Look for someone who has experience in your industry and who is not associated with your company, or the procurement process you are pursuing. This can help ensure that their feedback is unbiased.

Send your value proposition: Send your value proposition to the procurement professional and ask for their honest feedback. Be clear about the type of feedback you are looking for and the timeframe in which you need it.

Schedule a follow-up call: Once the procurement professional has had a chance to review your value proposition, schedule a call to discuss their feedback in more detail. This will allow you to ask questions and clarify any points of confusion.

Take notes: During the call, take notes on the procurement professional's feedback. Pay attention to any suggestions they make for improvement and any areas where they think your value proposition could be stronger.

Incorporate feedback: After the call, take some time to review the feedback you received and incorporate it into your value proposition. Be open to making changes and adjustments that will make your value proposition more compelling.

Remember, the goal of seeking feedback is to make your value proposition as strong as possible. Don't take any criticism personally, but instead, use it as an opportunity to improve your value proposition and increase your chances of winning the procurement process.

One way to make your value proposition stand out is by including unique services that your company provides at no extra cost. These services can set you apart from competitors and increase your chances of winning the contract.

To identify these unique services, start by researching your competitors and understanding what they offer. Look for gaps in their services that your company can fill. For example, if your competitors offer basic technical support, consider offering 24/7 technical support or a dedicated account manager for the duration of the contract.

Another approach is to analyze the needs of the agency or organization you are targeting. Identify areas where they may be facing challenges or where they have expressed specific needs in the past. You can then tailor your services to address these needs.

It's also important to ensure that the services you offer are feasible and realistic for your company to provide. Be sure to consider any additional resources or staff that may be required to deliver these services. Another approach is to look for services that are not typically offered by your competitors. This could be anything from training and education programs to ongoing support and maintenance. A great example of this would be a cleaning company that also offers pest control services. By offering these services at no extra cost, you can differentiate yourself from the competition and provide added value to the customer.

Finally, don't be afraid to propose services that the organization may not have considered or even knew existed. For example, if you are bidding on a contract for a hospital system, you could propose an innovative patient-tracking system that utilizes artificial intelligence and machine learning. While this may not have been on the organization's radar, it could provide significant value and improve patient outcomes.

When including these types of services in your value proposition, it's important to explain how they will benefit the customer and provide measurable results. This will help the organization understand the value of your proposal and increase your chances of winning the contract. Additionally, be prepared to provide further information and answer any questions the customer may have about these additional services.

Potential bidders need to be careful when promising additional services at no cost in their value proposition. While offering additional services can set a bidder apart from its competitors, it's crucial to ensure that these services can be provided at no cost.

Overpromising additional services can lead to disappointment and mistrust if the bidder is unable to deliver on their promises. This can harm the bidder's reputation and make it difficult to win future contracts with the same agency.

It's essential for bidders to fully understand their capabilities and resources before making promises of additional services at no cost. Bidders should also consider the potential costs and resources required to provide these services and ensure that they can be provided without sacrificing the quality of their core services.

It's better to under promise and overdeliver than to overpromise and underdeliver. Bidders should focus on highlighting their core strengths and services while being transparent about any additional services they may offer. This approach can build trust with the agency and increase the likelihood of winning the contract.

For the Hood

Listen up. If you wanna win government contracts, you gotta have the best product on the block, just like when you hugging the block. And that product is your value proposition. It's what sets you apart from the competition and shows why the government should choose you over everyone else.

But just like cooking up the perfect batch of that work, crafting a killer value proposition takes skill and know-how. You gotta understand your customer and know what they need and what they're looking for. Then, you gotta make sure you're offering something that nobody else can, whether it's a unique service or just an unbeatable price.

Listen up, fam. When you putting together your value proposition, make sure you ain't just talking a big game. You gotta come correct with what you can actually deliver. You don't wanna get caught up in overpromising and underdelivering. That's like selling someone some primo kush and then giving them a bag of reggie. You gonna get a bad rep real quick and the government ain't gonna wanna do business with you no more. Keep it real and make sure you can deliver the goods, otherwise you gonna get cut off from the bidding process faster than you can say "bid rejected."

So, put in the work and make sure you're creating a value proposition that's gonna make the government come back to you time and time again. Just like in the streets, the key to success is having the best product out there.

Yo, listen up! When it comes to creating a strong value proposition, you gotta make sure it's a hit with the customer. That's why you need to test it out, just like the local hustlers test out their new product on the addicts.

To test out your value proposition, you can start by presenting it to a select group of potential customers or procurement professionals. See how they react and ask for their honest feedback. If they're feeling it, you know you're on the right track. But if they're not feeling it, you gotta go back to the drawing board and come up with something better.

Think of it like this: You wouldn't just throw a new product out on the street without making sure it's good, right? Same goes for your value proposition. You gotta make sure it's gonna hit the spot before you start putting it out there.

And remember, just like with drugs, you don't wanna put out a bad batch. If your value proposition falls short, it could damage your reputation and make it harder for you to get in the game. So always keep testing and refining until you've got something that's truly dope. Pun intended.

Sample Value Proposition

Our company provides top-notch IT solutions that are tailored to meet the specific needs of your government agency. Our team of experts will work closely with you to develop and implement innovative strategies that will improve efficiency, reduce costs, and enhance the overall effectiveness of your operations. Our services are backed by our commitment to exceptional customer service and support, ensuring that you are always satisfied with the results. With our cutting-edge technology and unparalleled expertise, you can trust us to provide the solutions you need to succeed.

In addition to our top-notch IT solutions, we also offer additional services that will benefit your government agency. Our team can provide comprehensive training to your staff to ensure they are equipped with the skills necessary to effectively utilize our technology. We also offer ongoing maintenance and support to ensure that your systems are always running smoothly. Our team stays up-to-date with the latest advancements in the IT industry to ensure that your agency is utilizing the most advanced and innovative technology available. Furthermore, we will identify potential areas of improvement within your agency's operations that may require IT solutions that you may not have known you needed. By providing these additional services, we aim to ensure that our clients receive the maximum value from our IT solutions and remain at the forefront of their industry.

Practice Value Proposition

Value Add

Lesson IV

KNOW THY ENEMY
(Know your Competitors)

Knowing your competitors is a critical aspect of successful government contracting. Understanding who your competition is, what they offer, and how they position themselves in the market can help you differentiate your business, target your ideal customers, and ultimately win more contracts.

To start, research your competitors' business models, products, services, and pricing structures. Look for gaps in the market that they are not addressing and consider ways that your business can fill those gaps. This will help you identify unique selling points that you can emphasize in your marketing and value proposition.

Additionally, research your competitors' reputations in the industry. Look for customer reviews, ratings, and feedback on public forums, social media, and their websites. This will help you understand their strengths and weaknesses, and what customers appreciate or criticize about their services.

Understanding your competitors is a critical step in any business strategy, and it's no different in government contracting. To gain an advantage in the bidding process, you need to know your competitors inside and out. Beyond simply identifying who they are, you need to understand their strengths, weaknesses, and overall reputation in the industry.

One way to do this is by conducting thorough research on their online presence. Check out their websites and social media pages to see how they market themselves, what services they offer, and what sets them apart. Take note of any awards or recognitions they may have received, as well as any partnerships or collaborations they've established.

But don't stop there. To get a sense of how your competitors operate and how they are perceived in the market, you need to dig deeper. Look for customer reviews and feedback on public forums, social media, and their webs. Pay attention to what customers appreciate about their services, as well as what they criticize or complain about.

This research can help you identify areas where your competitors may be falling short and where you can offer better services. It can also help you identify opportunities to differentiate yourself and highlight your strengths in your bid proposal.

Another important aspect of researching your competitors is understanding their pricing strategies. Analyze their pricing structure and compare it to your own to ensure that you're offering competitive rates. This doesn't mean you should undercut them or engage in a price war, but rather that you should be aware of what your competitors are charging and how that may affect your pricing strategy.

It's also important to stay up-to-date on industry trends and news. Attending industry conferences and events, networking with other contractors and government officials, and following industry-specific publications and websites.

This will help you identify emerging market opportunities, stay ahead of the curve on new regulations and requirements, and adjust your business strategy accordingly.

Finally, don't forget to evaluate your strengths and weaknesses compared to your competitors. Consider conducting a SWOT analysis (Strengths, Weaknesses, Opportunities, and Threats) to identify areas where you excel and areas where you need to improve. This can help you position yourself more effectively in the market and differentiate yourself from your competitors.

A SWOT analysis is a strategic planning tool used to identify an organization's strengths, weaknesses, opportunities, and threats. It is a helpful tool to use when trying to evaluate your competition. By conducting a SWOT analysis, you can gain a better understanding of your competitors and how to position your organization to compete effectively.

The first step in conducting a SWOT analysis is to identify the strengths and weaknesses of your competitors. This can be done by researching their products or services, customer feedback, financial performance, marketing strategies, and employee skills and experience. By identifying their strengths and weaknesses, you can determine areas where your organization can compete or differentiate itself.

The next step is to identify opportunities and threats in the market. Opportunities can include new or emerging markets, changing customer needs, or advancements in technology. Threats can include economic downturns, new competitors, or changes in regulations. By identifying these opportunities and threats, you can adjust your strategy to take advantage of opportunities and mitigate potential threats.

By conducting a SWOT analysis, you can gain valuable insights into your competitors and the market. This information can help you make informed decisions about your organization's strategy and how to position yourself in the market. Ultimately, knowing your competition through a SWOT analysis can give you a competitive edge and help you succeed in the long term.

Not only should you be aware of their strengths and weaknesses, but you should also keep an eye on their business trends. If a competitor loses a contract with another government agency, it could provide you with an advantage.

Firstly, investigate why the competitor lost the contract. Were they unable to meet the agency's needs or provide the required level of service? Did they have any compliance issues or ethical violations that led to the termination of the contract? Understanding the reasons for their failure can help you avoid making the same mistakes and better prepare for your bid.

Secondly, analyze the gaps in the market that the competitor's loss creates. Are there any services or solutions that the agency still needs but the competitor was unable to provide? If so, you can use this information to tailor your bid and highlight your ability to meet those needs.

Thirdly, reach out to the agency that terminated the contract and offer your services. If they were dissatisfied with your competitor's work, they may be interested in exploring other options. Be sure to highlight your strengths and how you can address any concerns they may have had with your competitor.

When it comes to government contracting, agencies take a close look at a company's performance and compliance history. If a company has lost contracts with other government agencies due to issues such as poor performance or compliance violations, it can negatively impact its chances of winning future contracts.

As a potential bidder, it's important to investigate your competition's history of losing contracts with other agencies. This can provide valuable insights into any weaknesses or areas of concern that may need to be addressed in your bid proposal.

One way to gather this information is through the use of a Past Performance Information Retrieval System (PPIRS) report. This report provides information on a company's performance history, including any instances of contract terminations or non-compliance issues. Additionally, many government agencies include a form in their request for proposals (RFPs) that asks bidders to disclose whether they have ever had a contract terminated.

By researching your competition's performance history and leveraging this information in your bid proposal, you can highlight your strengths and demonstrate your company's ability to deliver high-quality services that meet or exceed the expectations of government agencies. This can give you a significant advantage in the bidding process and increase your chances of winning valuable government contracts.

Mentioning another company losing a contract in your bid proposal can be a tricky move, but if done tactfully, it can give you an advantage. By acknowledging the shortcomings of your competitors, you demonstrate that you understand the expectations of the agency and that you have a better understanding of how to meet them.

However, it's important to approach this topic with sensitivity and professionalism. Instead of openly criticizing the other company, focus on highlighting your strengths and how they set you apart. You might mention that you have experience working with similar agencies and that your track record demonstrates your ability to deliver on your promises.

If you do mention the other company, make sure you do your due diligence and research the reasons for their contract termination. If it was due to performance or compliance issues, be sure to emphasize your commitment to quality and compliance.

It's also important to keep in mind that the agency may not want to hear negative information about other companies, so use your judgment and be mindful of the tone and wording you use. If in doubt, seek feedback from a trusted procurement professional or legal advisor.

For the Hood

Yo! If you were trying to sell dinners from your home, you would need to know who your competition is. Same goes for government contracting, homie. You gotta do your research and find out who else is trying to get that contract.

First things first, find out who your competitors are. Check out their websites and social media pages. See what they're offering and how they're marketing themselves.

But that ain't all. You gotta know what makes you different from the competition. What unique flavor are you bringing to the table? Is it your grandma's secret recipe or your special spice blend? Same goes for government contracting, what sets you apart from the other companies? Do you offer faster turnaround times or more cost-effective solutions?

Don't be afraid to check out your competitors' reputations, too. A customer will gladly tell you when the food is nasty. Same goes for government contracting, if a company has a history of non-performance or compliance issues, you don't want to be associated with them.

Lastly, find out if your competition has any connections with the agency you're trying to contract with. You don't want to be up against someone who's got their foot in the door, you feel me? So, whether you're selling dinners from your home or trying to get that government contract, knowing your competition is key. Stay hungry and stay ahead of the game.

When it comes to knowing your competition, it ain't just about gathering intel - you gotta make sure that what you're getting is accurate. There's no use in basing your strategy on false information, it'll only lead to your downfall.

Think about it like this: if you're selling dinners from your home and you hear that your competition has the best mac and cheese in the game, you better make sure that's true before you start tweaking your recipe. You don't wanna end up adding extra cheese and losing money just to compete with a rumor.

Same goes for government contracting. If you hear that a competitor has a bad reputation, you can't just take that as fact. You gotta do your research and make sure the information is legit. That way, you can use it to your advantage and edge out the competition.

So, make sure you double-check your sources and confirm the information you gather. Don't fall victim to fake news, 'cause in the end, it'll only hurt you. Stay sharp and stay on top of your game.

Competition ain't always a bad thing. Sometimes it can even be an opportunity to get that bread without going through the whole bidding process. Lemme break it down for ya.

Say you got your eye on a government contract, but you know there's already a big player in the game. Instead of trying to go head-to-head with them, you might wanna consider offering to subcontract with them. That way, you get a piece of the pie without all the stress and hassle of bidding for the whole contract yourself.

And even if you do decide to bid against them, it's important to remember that competition can push you to step up your game and bring your A-game. It can motivate you to come up with new and innovative ideas and ultimately improve your chances of winning that contract.

But hold up, before you start strategizing, make sure you do your homework on the competition. Check out their strengths and weaknesses, their reputation in the game, and their relationships with the government agency. Once you got all that info, you can figure out if sub-contracting is the move, or if you wanna go all in and compete for the contract. Remember SWOT Analysis? Not to be confused with SWAT. We all know that one.

Sample SWOT Analysis

SWOT Analysis for XYZ Cleaning Company:

Strengths:

Experienced and trained cleaning staff

Reputation for providing quality services

Wide range of cleaning services offered, including residential, commercial, and industrial cleaning

Flexible scheduling options to accommodate clients' needs

Use of eco-friendly and non-toxic cleaning products

Weaknesses:

Limited marketing and advertising budget

High competition in the cleaning industry

Reliance on a small number of large clients for a significant portion of revenue

Dependence on a small team of employees to deliver services

Opportunities:

Expansion of services to include specialized cleaning services, such as carpet and upholstery cleaning

Targeting new markets, such as medical facilities and schools

Developing strategic partnerships with complementary businesses, such as pest control companies or landscaping services

Establishing an online presence and increasing digital marketing efforts

Threats:

Economic downturns and budget cuts leading to reduced demand for cleaning services

Emergence of new competitors with lower pricing or stronger marketing strategies

Changing regulations and requirements for cleaning products and methods

Negative online reviews and word-of-mouth publicity about unsatisfactory services.

Practice SWOT Analysis

Strengths:

Weaknesses:

Opportunities:

Threats:

Lesson V

GET ON PAPI'S CONTACT LIST
(Build Strong Relationships)

Bid sites like Bidnet and Bonfire are online platforms that allow businesses to access bidding opportunities from various government agencies and large contractors. These sites can be useful for businesses looking to expand their reach and gain more exposure to potential contracts.

To register with these sites, businesses typically need to create an account and provide information about their company, such as their size, location, and industry. Once registered, businesses can search for relevant bidding opportunities and submit their proposals online.

Registering with bid sites can be a great way to get on an agency's contact list, as these sites often work with multiple government agencies and contractors. By submitting proposals through these platforms, businesses can increase their chances of being considered for contracts and build relationships with agencies and contractors.

It's important to note, however, that not all agencies and contractors use bid sites. It's still important for businesses to do their research and reach out to agencies and contractors directly to inquire about their procurement processes and get on their contact list.

In addition to bid sites, businesses can also register with agencies and contractors through their respective procurement portals. These portals typically require businesses to provide similar information about their company, but also often require more specific details about their products or services.

In addition to registering with bid sites like Bidnet and Bonfire, bidders must register directly with the government agency they're interested in contracting with. Registering on the agency's website also registers you as a vendor with that agency, increasing your chances of being contacted for future opportunities.

To register on an agency's website, you should first visit the agency's procurement page and look for instructions on how to become a vendor. Typically, you'll need to provide information such as your company's name, contact information, W-9, corporate filing, and a brief description of the goods or services you offer.

Make sure to keep your vendor profile up-to-date and accurate, as agencies often use these profiles to search for potential vendors. Additionally, some agencies may require you to submit certain documents or certifications to qualify for certain contracts.

By registering directly with the agency, you demonstrate your interest and commitment to working with them, and you'll have a greater chance of being notified of new opportunities that may not be listed on bid sites. It's important to stay proactive and keep an eye out for new opportunities, so don't be afraid to reach out to the agency periodically to inquire about potential contracts or to update your vendor profile.

Agencies may change the bidding site they use, which means that vendors who are only registered on a specific bidding site may miss out on potential opportunities. For example, as a municipality grows, it may change from using a third-party bidding site such as Bidnet and opt to release bids on its website. By registering with the agency directly, bidders can ensure that they are always on the agency's radar, regardless of which bidding site they use.

If you're looking to do business with the government, you need to know where to go to find opportunities to bid on contracts. One great resource for finding state and local government procurement websites is the NIGP website. NIGP stands for the National Institute of Governmental Purchasing, and its website is a wealth of information for anyone looking to do business with the government.

Once you're on the NIGP website, look for the "State and Provinces Procurement Websites" section. This directory will give you a list of all the different state governments and regions across the country. Click on your state to find your local state-run procurement website.

"State and Provinces Procurement Websites" serve as a catch-all for each state or province, providing a centralized location for government agencies to post bids and solicitations. They provide access to all open bids and solicitations, as well as notifications of new opportunities. Additionally, it's important to regularly check these websites as agencies may change the websites, they use to post bids and solicitations.

Setting up a dedicated email address to receive bid notifications can save you time and hassle when it comes to responding to bid opportunities. It's important to keep all bid notifications in one place, so you can easily track and manage them.

When you register on bidding websites or with agencies, make sure to set up notifications for future bids. This way, you'll receive an email or alert when a new opportunity arises. Doing this on every site you register with is crucial, so you don't miss out on any potential bids.

A dedicated email address also helps you filter out spam and prioritize bid notifications. You can easily flag bid opportunities as important and keep track of them separately from other emails.

Remember to check your dedicated email regularly and respond to bid opportunities promptly. Missing a bid deadline can result in disqualification, so staying on top of notifications and submitting bids on time is important.

Sub-contracting can be a valuable way to get your foot in the door with government agencies and large contractors. By reaching out to them and proposing a partnership, you could land a contract that you wouldn't have been able to secure on your own.

To get on sub-contractor contact lists, start by researching and identifying companies that may need your services as a sub-contractor. Reach out to them directly and explain your capabilities and how your services could complement theirs. Networking events and industry conferences can also be great places to meet potential partners and make valuable connections.

It's important to keep in mind that subcontracting relationships should be mutually beneficial and profitable for both parties. Make sure to thoroughly vet any potential partners and have clear expectations and terms laid out in a written agreement. With the right sub-contracting partnership, you can grow your business and gain valuable experience working with government agencies and large contractors.

When you are a small business looking to become a sub-contractor for a larger company bidding on government contracts, it is important to ensure that your company is properly registered and identified in the bid documents. One way to accomplish this is by submitting a subcontractor affidavit along with the larger company's bid.

A sub-contractor affidavit is a legal document that certifies the relationship between the larger company and your small business. It provides details such as your company name, address, and contact information, as well as the scope of work that your business will perform under the contract. By including this affidavit with the bid, the larger company ensures that your business is locked in as a sub-contractor if they are awarded the contract.

For example, let's say you own a hauling company that specializes in debris removal, and a street repair company is bidding on a government contract that involves both debris removal and street repair. The street repair company may not be allowed to bid on the contract without a local small business as a sub-contractor for the hauling work. By submitting a subcontractor affidavit with their bid that includes your company's information, the street repair company ensures that your business is identified as the sub-contractor for hauling work if they are awarded the contract.

Make sure that you provide accurate and up-to-date information in the subcontractor affidavit. Any discrepancies or errors could result in your company being disqualified from the contract or facing legal action. It is also important to stay in communication with the larger company throughout the bidding process and to follow up with them after the contract is awarded to ensure that everything is in order and that your small business is properly listed as a subcontractor.

A pre-bid conference is a meeting held by the agency or organization issuing the bid, usually before the bid submission deadline. This meeting provides an opportunity for interested vendors to ask questions, seek clarification on any issues, and gain a better understanding of the project or contract requirements.

Attending a pre-bid conference can be highly beneficial for vendors as it allows them to meet with agency representatives and other potential vendors. It provides an opportunity to network, make connections, and learn about potential subcontracting opportunities. This can also help vendors gain a better understanding of their competition, as they can observe who else is interested in bidding on the project or contract.

Vendors who attend pre-bid conferences should come prepared with questions and a solid understanding of their capabilities and experience. They should also be ready to introduce themselves to other vendors and agency representatives and make an effort to establish relationships and partnerships with other businesses. By making themselves known and building connections, vendors can increase their chances of success in the bidding process and potentially secure valuable subcontracting opportunities.

For the Hood

Yo, if you're trying to get in on the government contracting game, you gotta know how to play it. And one of the first things you gotta do is get registered on the bidding sites. These sites are like hotspots for government contract opportunities. You can find all kinds of bids here, from construction to IT to janitorial services. It's like a candy store for vendors, and you don't wanna miss out on the treats.

But it's not just about registering on the bidding sites. You gotta make sure you also register as a vendor with the agencies themselves. This is how they know you're legit and ready to do business. It's like getting your name in the game, and you gotta do it if you wanna win.

And let me tell you, registering on these sites and with the agencies is crucial. If you're not on the list, you're not getting invites. You gotta be in the know to get the dough, you feel me? And that means signing up for notifications of future bids so you're always in the loop.

Now, I know what you're thinking. "How am I gonna keep up with all these notifications?" Don't worry, I got you. Set up a special email just for bid notifications. That way, you won't miss a single opportunity. And make sure you're checking it regularly because you never know when a new bid might pop up.

But it's not just about signing up and waiting for the invites to roll in. You gotta be proactive, too. Attend pre-bid meetings and introduce yourself to potential subcontractors. Let them know who you are and what you can bring to the table. This is how you build relationships and make connections that can lead to bigger opportunities down the line.

And speaking of subcontractors, you gotta make sure you're on their radar, too. A lot of bigger companies are required to have a local small business as a subcontractor, so make sure they know you're out there and ready to work. Submit those sub-contractor affidavits with your bids so you're locked in and ready to go when the contract is awarded.

So, to sum it up: register, sign up for notifications, attend pre-bid meetings, and make connections with potential subcontractors. It's all about getting your name out there and making sure people know what you can do. Get on it, and you'll be on your way to government contract success.

Lesson VI

ASSEMBLE YA TEAM
(Build a Strong Team)

Having adequate staffing is crucial to the success of any contract. Before submitting a bid, it's important to carefully evaluate the scope of work and determine the appropriate level of staffing required to complete the work on time and within budget. This includes not only the number of personnel needed but also their specific skills and qualifications.

Once the contract has been awarded, it's important to ensure that there are enough staff members on hand to handle the workload. This may require hiring additional staff or reassigning existing staff members from other projects. It's important to be proactive in this regard, as a shortage of staff can lead to missed deadlines, cost overruns, and a loss of confidence in your ability to perform.

In addition to having enough staff members, it's important to have a backup plan in case of unexpected absences or turnover. This can be achieved by cross-training staff members or by having a pool of qualified candidates who can be called upon at a moment's notice. By being prepared for any eventuality, you can ensure that the contract is completed on time and to the satisfaction of the client.

It's also important to ensure that staff members have the necessary tools and resources to do their jobs effectively. This includes not only physical tools such as computers and software but also training and support to ensure that staff members can use these tools to their fullest potential. Providing ongoing training and professional development opportunities can also help to keep staff members engaged and motivated.

Another key factor in ensuring adequate staffing is to monitor staff performance and productivity. This can be achieved by setting clear expectations, providing regular feedback and coaching, and implementing performance metrics to track progress. By providing ongoing support and feedback, you can help staff members to improve their performance and achieve their goals.

It's also important to foster a positive work environment that encourages teamwork and collaboration. This can be achieved by promoting open communication, providing opportunities for staff members to work together on projects, and recognizing and rewarding outstanding performance. By creating a supportive and collaborative work environment, you can build a strong team that is capable of achieving great things.

In some cases, it may be necessary to outsource certain tasks or functions to third-party vendors or contractors. When doing so, it's important to carefully evaluate the vendor's qualifications and track record and to establish clear expectations and performance metrics. It's also important to ensure that the vendor's staff members have the necessary skills and resources to complete the work to the satisfaction of the client.

It's important to be flexible and adaptable in the face of changing circumstances. This may require adjusting staffing levels, reallocating resources, or changing the scope of work to better meet the needs of the client. By being responsive and flexible, you can ensure that the contract is completed on time and to the satisfaction of all parties involved.

When a company contracts with the government, it is important to understand the labor and management commitment that is being made. The government is entrusting the company to provide a specific service or product, and it is the responsibility of the company to fulfill that commitment.

Failing to fulfill the terms of the contract can have serious consequences. For example, if a company is unable to meet its obligations, it may be forced to forfeit its bond funds or face legal action from the government. In some cases, the company may even lose the contract altogether.

To avoid these consequences, it is important to carefully consider the labor and management commitment that will be required before entering into a government contract. Most municipalities will not pull a contract of sue the moment an issue arises. Most municipalities will provide a "notice to cure" to the vendor and allow them to correct the action.

In government contracting, a "notice to cure" is a formal written communication that is issued to a contractor who is not meeting the requirements of their contract. The notice typically identifies specific areas where the contractor is failing to meet the requirements and provides a timeframe within which the contractor must take corrective action. The notice may also outline the consequences of failing to cure the identified deficiencies, such as termination of the contract or withholding of payment. The purpose of a notice to cure is to allow the contractor to address the deficiencies and bring their performance up to the required standard.

Ultimately, the key to fulfilling a government contract is a strong commitment to quality, efficiency, and excellence. By understanding the labor and management requirements, investing in the necessary resources and personnel, and staying focused on the goal of delivering top-notch service, companies can succeed in the challenging world of government contracting.

A contractor's team goes beyond just their employees. While having a strong and capable workforce is certainly important, some other professionals and entities are crucial to the success of a contracting business. These may include accountants, bankers, insurance professionals, and others who play an important role in running a legitimate and successful business.

For example, having a skilled and reliable accountant can help a contractor manage their finances and ensure that they are meeting all tax and regulatory requirements. A good banker or banking relationship can provide access to financing and credit, which can be especially important for small businesses that may struggle to obtain financing through traditional means. Insurance professionals can help contractors manage risk and ensure that they have appropriate coverage for their operations.

In addition to these professionals, a contractor's team may also include other key partners and collaborators. For example, if a contractor frequently works with subcontractors or other partners, having a strong network of these entities can be crucial to successfully bid on and completing contracts. Likewise, having strong relationships with suppliers and vendors can ensure that the contractor has access to the materials and equipment they need to perform their work.

Establishing strong supplier relationships is crucial for any contractor looking to succeed in government contracting. When working on a project, contractors rely heavily on their suppliers to provide the necessary materials and equipment to complete the job. Therefore, it is important to develop a good working relationship with suppliers to ensure timely delivery of quality materials at a reasonable price.

One important aspect of supplier relationships is price negotiation. In many cases, suppliers may offer lower prices to contractors with whom they have a long-standing relationship. This can be especially beneficial for contractors who purchase large volumes of materials regularly, as they can negotiate bulk discounts and other favorable terms.

Another benefit of building strong supplier relationships is that suppliers are often willing to go above and beyond to meet the needs of their preferred customers. This can include expedited delivery times, specialized services, or even customized materials. Having a strong relationship with a supplier can also help contractors avoid potential supply chain disruptions and delays.

In addition to price negotiations and custom services, building strong supplier relationships can also provide contractors with access to valuable industry knowledge and insights. Suppliers can provide information on the latest materials and technologies, as well as advice on best practices for using and installing them. This information can be invaluable in helping contractors stay ahead of the curve and remain competitive in the market.

When building supplier relationships, it is important to maintain open communication and a willingness to work together to solve any issues that may arise. Contractors should establish clear expectations and regularly communicate their needs and deadlines. Suppliers should also be kept up to date on any changes to the project scope or timeline.

In conclusion, building a strong team is crucial to success in government contracting. It goes beyond just having a talented and dedicated staff. You must also have strong relationships with key partners, such as accountants, bankers, insurance professionals, and others who help keep your business running smoothly. It's important to understand the labor and management commitment you are making when you contract with the government and to have a plan in place to fulfill those obligations.

Additionally, having a reliable supplier base is essential to meeting contract requirements and staying within budget. This often means developing strong relationships with suppliers, negotiating prices based on a history of purchasing and consistent business, and ensuring that your supply chain is secure and reliable.

Finally, it's important to recognize that your team's success is not just about meeting contractual obligations, but also about creating a positive reputation for your business within the industry. Building trust and respect among your peers, clients, and vendors can lead to more opportunities for growth and success in the future.

Overall, building a strong team takes time, effort, and dedication. But with the right approach and a commitment to excellence, you can assemble a team that can meet the demands of even the most challenging government contracts.

For the Hood

Yo, when it comes to winning government contracts, it ain't just about the boss or the company. You gotta have a squad that's strong and tight, like Jay-Z and Beyonce. You need more than just employees, you need a team that includes your accountant, banker, insurance professional, and other key players that help you run a tight ship.

But it ain't just about having a good team, you gotta make sure you got enough people on deck to support the contract. You can't be out here promising the world and then not be able to deliver. If you ain't got enough staff to handle the workload, you gonna end up getting hit with a "notice to cure" and that's gonna mess up your whole game.

And speaking of the game, you gotta have a solid labor and management commitment. When you contract with the government, you making a serious commitment. If you can't deliver, you gonna lose bond funds or even the contract itself. That's why you gotta make sure you understand the labor and management commitment you're making before you sign on the dotted line.

You also gotta have tight relationships with your suppliers. Sometimes it's all about who you know and how long you've been doing business with them. Negotiating prices for materials can be a result of a lengthy relationship and the amount of materials purchased. So make sure you keep those relationships tight and on point.

Keep in mind, it ain't just about getting the contract, it's about building relationships. You never know who you might need to call on in the future.

And who knows, maybe one day you'll be the big player and someone else will be calling you for help. It's all about having respect, staying professional, and building that team to get the job done right.

Lesson VII

MAKE AN OFFER THEY CAN'T REFUSE
(Demonstrate Technical Expertise and Competitive Pricing)

A technical proposal is a document that outlines a company's plan to solve a problem or fulfill a need for a government agency or other client. This proposal is typically written in response to a Request for Proposal (RFP) or a Request for Quote (RFQ) and outlines the technical aspects of the project, including the methodology, materials, and timelines. The purpose of a technical proposal is to demonstrate that the company has the technical expertise and resources necessary to successfully complete the project.

To write a technical proposal, there are several steps that a company should take:

Review the RFP or RFQ carefully: Before starting to write the proposal, it is essential to read the RFP or RFQ thoroughly to understand the requirements, deadlines, and evaluation criteria. Develop a project team: Identify the key personnel who will be involved in the project and assign specific roles and responsibilities.

Conduct a needs assessment: Conduct research and gather information to fully understand the needs and objectives of the agency or client. This will enable the company to tailor the proposal to meet those specific needs.

Outline the technical approach: The technical approach should outline how the company plans to solve the problem or fulfill the need outlined in the RFP or RFQ. This should include details on the methodology, materials, and timelines.

Provide a work breakdown structure: A work breakdown structure is a detailed breakdown of the project into smaller, more manageable tasks. This provides the agency or client with a clear understanding of the scope of the project and how it will be executed.

Demonstrate technical expertise: The proposal should demonstrate the company's technical expertise and resources, including any relevant experience, certifications, or partnerships.

Address potential issues: The proposal should also address any potential issues or challenges that may arise during the project and provide a plan to mitigate those risks.

Highlight value proposition: Finally, the proposal should highlight the company's value proposition, including any competitive advantages or cost savings that it can offer.

Overall, a technical proposal should be well-organized, concise, and written in clear, jargon-free language. It should also be visually appealing, with diagrams, charts, and other graphics used to help illustrate key points.

Writing a strong technical proposal can be a time-consuming process, but it is essential for securing government contracts and other business opportunities. By following these steps and dedicating the necessary resources, companies can increase their chances of success and demonstrate their technical expertise to potential clients.

When it comes to writing a technical proposal, it is important to note that the same proposal can be used for different bids with just a few tweaks to the information presented. This is because most government agencies and large contractors use a standard format for technical proposals, which means that the basic structure and content of the proposal remain the same, regardless of the specific project being bid on.

The key to successfully reusing a technical proposal is to tailor the content of the proposal to the specific needs of the agency or contractor you are bidding with. This means that you should pay close attention to the specific requirements outlined in the bid solicitation and make sure that your proposal addresses each of these requirements clearly and concisely.

For example, if you are bidding on a project that requires expertise in a specific area, such as IT or engineering, you may need to highlight your experience and qualifications in this area in more detail than you would for a project that does not have this requirement. Similarly, if the agency or contractor is looking for a specific type of technology or equipment, you may need to highlight your experience and expertise in working with this technology or equipment.

The key to successfully reusing a technical proposal is to ensure that the proposal is customized to the specific needs of the agency or contractor you are bidding with. This means that you need to take the time to carefully review the bid solicitation and any other relevant materials and then use this information to tailor your proposal to the specific needs of the project.

In addition to customizing the content of your proposal, it is also important to make sure that your proposal is presented clearly and professionally. This means using a consistent format and style throughout the proposal, and including any relevant supporting documentation, such as resumes, project summaries, or letters of recommendation.

To ensure that your proposal stands out from the competition, you may also want to consider incorporating visual elements, such as charts, graphs, or images, that help to illustrate the key points of your proposal in a visually compelling way.

A technical proposal is a detailed document that outlines the approach and methodology for completing a project or contract. The purpose of a technical proposal is to demonstrate to the client that the bidder has the knowledge, skills, and experience to successfully execute the project. Several key components should be included in the technical proposal to make it effective.

Introduction: The introduction should provide an overview of the project and the bidder's understanding of the client's needs. It should establish credibility and convey enthusiasm for the project.

Project Scope and Objectives: This section should clearly define the project scope and objectives. It should provide a detailed description of what the bidder will do and what the expected outcomes are.

Approach and Methodology: This is perhaps the most important section of the technical proposal. It should provide a detailed explanation of how the bidder plans to approach the project, including the methodology, tools, and techniques that will be used.

Timelines and Deliverables: This section should provide a timeline of the project, including major milestones and deliverables. It should demonstrate the bidder's ability to manage the project and meet deadlines.

Qualifications and Experience: This section should provide information about the bidder's qualifications and experience, including relevant certifications, education, and work experience. It should demonstrate the bidder's expertise in the field.

Project Team: This section should introduce the members of the bidder's project team and provide information about their qualifications and experience. It should demonstrate that the bidder has a strong team in place to execute the project.

Budget and Pricing: This section should provide a detailed breakdown of the costs associated with the project, including materials, labor, and other expenses. It should demonstrate that the bidder has a clear understanding of the project requirements and can provide a competitive price.

Appendices: This section can include additional information that supports the proposal, such as resumes, work samples, or case studies.

A technical proposal is a critical document that can make or break a bid for a government contract. It's essential to ensure that it's well-written and presents all of the required information clearly and concisely. While creating a technical proposal can be a challenging and time-consuming process, it's well worth the effort to win a lucrative government contract.

Having someone review your technical proposal before submission can provide valuable feedback and help you identify any areas that need improvement. An outside perspective can often spot errors or inconsistencies that you might have missed, as well as provide suggestions for improving the overall flow and readability of the document.

Ultimately, the goal of a technical proposal is to convince the agency evaluating the bids that your company has the knowledge, skills, and experience to deliver the best solution to meet their needs. By including all of the key components, such as a clear understanding of the project, a detailed project plan, qualifications, and experience, and a thorough budget and pricing strategy, you can increase your chances of winning the contract.

Remember, the technical proposal is just one aspect of the overall bid package. Be sure to also address any additional requirements or documentation, such as a pricing proposal, proof of insurance, or references. By providing a complete and well-organized bid package, you demonstrate your company's professionalism and attention to detail, which can give you a competitive advantage in the bidding process.

In summary, writing a technical proposal requires careful planning, attention to detail, and an understanding of the agency's needs and requirements. It's essential to use the key components discussed in this chapter and to have someone review the proposal before submission. With these elements in place, you can create a winning technical proposal and increase your chances of winning a government contract.

Cost proposals are an essential component of the bidding process for government contracts. While technical proposals highlight your capabilities and expertise, cost proposals outline the financial aspects of your proposal. The goal of a cost proposal is to provide the government agency with an accurate estimate of the cost of your proposed work. This estimate should include all costs associated with the project, including labor, materials, equipment, and overhead expenses.

To create a successful cost proposal, you should have a clear understanding of the scope of work and the requirements of the contract. You should also have a comprehensive understanding of the pricing structure of the industry and the cost of the materials and equipment you will be using. The cost proposal should include a detailed breakdown of all costs associated with the project. This should include direct costs, such as labor and materials, as well as indirect costs, such as overhead expenses.

To create a competitive cost proposal, it's important to accurately estimate your costs while also being mindful of the budget of the agency. You should strive to provide a fair and reasonable price while also making a profit for your company. It's also important to include any cost-saving measures or efficiencies that you can provide. For example, if you have a process or equipment that can complete the work more efficiently or with less waste, this should be highlighted in the cost proposal.

Additionally, you should be prepared to justify any costs that may be higher than the industry standard. This may include specialized equipment or materials that are necessary for the project. Providing detailed explanations and justifications for these costs can help to build credibility with the agency.

Finally, it's important to ensure that your cost proposal aligns with your technical proposal. Your cost proposal should reflect the scope of work and requirements outlined in your technical proposal. Any discrepancies between the two may raise red flags for the agency. By providing a fair and reasonable price and highlighting any cost-saving measures or efficiencies, you can create a competitive and successful cost proposal.

When submitting a proposal for a government contract, it's essential to pay attention to all the dates on the solicitation document. This includes the bid submission date, the pre-bid meeting date, and the date to submit questions in writing. Each of these dates can have an impact on the cost proposal.

Firstly, the bid submission date is the most critical date to consider. This is the deadline for submitting your proposal and missing it can mean your bid is disqualified. It's essential to carefully review the solicitation document to ensure that you understand the bid submission requirements and have all necessary information prepared in advance.

Secondly, the pre-bid meeting is an opportunity for bidders to ask questions about the project, clarify requirements, and gain a better understanding of what the agency is looking for in a proposal.

Attending this meeting is highly recommended, as it can provide valuable insight that can be used to refine the cost proposal.

Thirdly, the date to submit questions in writing is equally important. This is the deadline for submitting any questions or clarifications you may have about the project to the agency. Submitting your questions in writing ensures that you have a clear record of your inquiries and the agency's responses, which can be used to support your cost proposal.

When preparing your cost proposal, it's essential to keep all these dates in mind. It's also worth noting that agencies may require specific formats or templates for the cost proposal. It's important to carefully review the solicitation document to ensure that your proposal meets all formatting and submission requirements.

When submitting a bid proposal for a government contract, it is important to ensure that all legal documents are completed accurately and submitted on time. These documents are usually attached as an appendix to the solicitation and include information such as a company's legal status, tax identification number, non-collusion affidavit, and immigration form.

It is essential to carefully review the solicitation and make sure that all required documents are included in the bid package. Missing or incomplete legal documents can result in a bid being disqualified or rejected, even if the technical proposal and cost proposal are strong.

In addition, some legal documents may need to be notarized or completed by third parties, such as a certified public accountant or attorney when financial statements are required. Documents such as subcontractor affidavits should be completed and included as well. It is important to allow enough time to gather these documents and have them completed before the bid submission deadline.

One common legal document that may be required is a certificate of insurance, which provides proof of liability and other types of insurance coverage. This document may need to be obtained from an insurance provider and should be reviewed carefully to ensure that it meets the requirements outlined in the solicitation.

Another important legal document is a bid bond or performance bond, which is a type of insurance that guarantees a bidder will enter into a contract if they are awarded the project. These bonds may be required by the government agency and must be obtained from a surety company.

Submitting a bid proposal for a government agency requires paying attention to how the agency wants the proposal to be submitted. It's important to read the solicitation carefully to determine if the agency wants the proposal delivered in person, by mail, or uploaded on an online platform. Some agencies may require the technical and cost proposal to be in separate envelopes or files, so it's crucial to pay attention to these details.

If the agency wants the proposal to be submitted in person, it's important to note the specific location and time for submission. It may also be helpful to arrive early to avoid any delays or unforeseen circumstances. In addition, be sure to have multiple copies of the proposal to ensure that the agency receives all necessary documents.

For agencies that require the proposal to be submitted by mail, it's important to consider the delivery timeline to ensure that the proposal arrives before the deadline. It's also important to pay attention to the specific address and formatting requirements for the submission, such as the use of certified mail or other delivery methods.

For online submissions, it's important to follow the agency's instructions carefully and ensure that all required documents are uploaded in the correct format. Some agencies may require specific software or tools to be used for submission, so be sure to download and install these in advance.

Regardless of the submission method, it's important to ensure that all legal documents and required forms are completed and submitted correctly. Some documents may require notarization or third-party signatures, so be sure to allow enough time for these processes.

It's important not to wait until the last minute to submit your proposal. Give yourself enough time to review the submission requirements and make any necessary adjustments. If the agency requires in-person delivery, make sure you obtain a receipt as proof of submission. Don't take any chances with the delivery process, as a missed deadline could mean automatic disqualification. By planning and ensuring that all submission requirements are met, you can improve your chances of winning the contract.

For the Hood

Listen! It's time to talk about cost and technical proposals. When you're bidding on a government contract, you gotta come correct with your proposal. It's gotta be tight and on-point to get that contract. Here's what you need to know.

First things first, you gotta pay attention to the dates. The bid submission date, pre-bid meeting date, and the date to submit questions in writing are all important. Make sure you know when these dates are and don't miss 'em. They can affect your cost proposal, so don't be slacking.

Next, you gotta complete all the legal documents that are normally attached as an appendix in the solicitation. This includes any documents that need to be notarized or completed by third parties. You don't wanna be missing any of these documents or you might as well kiss that contract goodbye.

Once you've got all your paperwork in order, it's time to turn in your proposal. Some agencies want the proposals delivered in person with the technical and cost proposal in different envelopes and several copies. Others may require the bid to be uploaded on an online platform. Make sure you know how the agency wants the proposal submitted.

And whatever you do, don't wait until the last day to submit. Give yourself plenty of time to get that proposal in on time. And if you do deliver it in person, make sure you get a receipt.

Now, let's talk about the technical proposal. This is where you show off your skills and expertise. You gotta show the agency that you know what you're doing and that you're the best choice for the job. Here are the key components of a technical proposal:

1. Cover page
2. Table of contents
3. Executive summary
4. Company overview
5. Technical approach and methodology
6. Project management plan
7. Key personnel resumes
8. Work plan and schedule
9. Quality control plan
10. Past performance references
11. Certifications and qualifications
12. Attachments and appendices

When you're writing your technical proposal, make sure you're addressing all the points in the solicitation. Don't miss anything. And don't be afraid to show off your skills and expertise.

Now, let's talk about the cost proposal. This is where you lay out your pricing. You gotta make sure you're pricing your services competitively but also making sure you're making a profit. Here are the key components of a cost proposal:

1. Labor category descriptions
2. Labor rates
3. Materials and equipment pricing
4. Indirect costs
5. Profit/fee

When you're writing your cost proposal, make sure you're following the format and instructions in the solicitation. And make sure your pricing is competitive but also makes sense for your business.

Finally, don't forget to have someone review your proposal before you submit it. You don't want any errors or mistakes that could cost you the contract. And always keep in mind that completing the required paperwork and submitting it on time is just as important as the proposal itself.

Sample Technical Proposal

Our company, Clean Sweep Janitorial Services, is pleased to submit this technical proposal in response to the City of Gotham's solicitation for janitorial services for its municipal buildings. With over 10 years of experience, our team is confident that we can provide the highest quality janitorial services to the City of Gotham. Our proposal provides a comprehensive plan that outlines our ability to deliver services that meet or exceed your expectations.

Scope of Work: We understand that the City of Gotham requires a wide range of janitorial services for its municipal buildings, and we are prepared to provide these services with the utmost care and attention. Our scope of work includes daily cleaning, floor care, carpet cleaning, window washing, and restroom cleaning. Additionally, we will ensure that all supplies and equipment necessary for the job are readily available and that all employees are trained on the proper use and handling of equipment.

Methodology: Our methodology is simple yet effective. We will assign a dedicated team to your municipal buildings that will be responsible for the daily cleaning and maintenance of the facilities. This team will be supervised by a project manager who will oversee all aspects of the job and ensure that it is completed to your satisfaction. Our employees will be trained on all aspects of the job, including proper use and handling of equipment, safety procedures, and customer service.

Staffing: Our team consists of experienced janitorial professionals who are committed to providing the highest quality of service. All employees are background-checked, drug-tested, and trained to the highest industry standards. We provide ongoing training to ensure that our team members are up-to-date on the latest cleaning techniques and equipment.

Equipment and Supplies: We will provide all necessary equipment and supplies for the job, including cleaning solutions, trash bags, and paper products. We use only environmentally-friendly cleaning products and equipment, ensuring that your facilities are cleaned safely and responsibly.

Quality Control: We believe that quality control is a critical component of our service. We will conduct regular inspections to ensure that our team is performing to the highest standards. Additionally, we will provide you with a detailed report outlining our activities, including the work performed and any issues that may have arisen.

Customer Service: Our commitment to customer service is unwavering. We understand that communication is key to a successful partnership, and we will keep you informed throughout the entire process. We will provide you with a dedicated point of contact who will be available to answer any questions or concerns that you may have.

Pricing: We understand that price is an important factor in your decision-making process. Our pricing is competitive, and we believe that our comprehensive approach to janitorial services provides excellent value for your investment.

Conclusion: In conclusion, Clean Sweep Janitorial Services is the ideal choice for the City of Gotham's janitorial needs. Our technical proposal outlines our commitment to providing high-quality service that is both reliable and affordable. We look forward to the opportunity to serve the City of Gotham and contribute to its continued success.

Sample Cost Proposal

Name of Company: Clean Sweep Janitorial Services

Project Name: ABC Federal Building Janitorial Services

Date of Proposal: May 1, 2023

Scope of Work:

Clean Sweep Janitorial Services (CSJS) is pleased to submit a cost proposal for providing janitorial services to the ABC Federal Building. The scope of work includes daily cleaning of all offices, hallways, restrooms, and common areas, as well as periodic deep cleaning of carpets and floors.

Pricing:

CSJS proposes a total price of $180,000 for the initial one-year contract period, with an option to renew for up to three additional one-year periods at the same price. The breakdown of the pricing is as follows:

Daily cleaning services (Monday through Friday, excluding holidays): $150,000 per year

Deep cleaning services (quarterly): $10,000 per year

Supplies and equipment: $20,000 per year

Payment Terms:

CSJS requires payment monthly, with payment due within 30 days of receipt of the invoice. A late payment fee of 1.5% per month will be added to any unpaid balance after 30 days.

Assumptions:

This cost proposal is based on the following assumptions:

The total square footage of the ABC Federal Building is 50,000 square feet

The current condition of the building is average, with no major cleaning or repair needs

CSJS will provide all necessary equipment and supplies for the cleaning services, except toilet paper, paper towels, and hand soap, which will be provided by the ABC Federal Building

Bonus Game

Before we close Chapter VII, let's talk about the new muscle on the block. AI will not win the contract for you; it will carry the weight so your strategy can breathe. Imagine a tireless junior who types blisteringly fast, skims a thousand pages without blinking, and never asks for coffee. Useful, powerful, not in charge. You still choose the plays, you still sign the bid, and you still own the outcome. Keep the golden rule close: a human stays in the loop. Let the system draft, but you decide what lives in the book and what dies on the cutting-room floor.

Here's how to put that muscle to work inside your proposal workflow without violating the laws of gravity or procurement. Start by feeding the entire solicitation package (RFP or RFQ), every addendum, and each attachment that might bend scope into an AI that can read documents. Your first goal is clarity. You want a clean summary of the Statement of Work as it appears in Section C, rendered as plain, traceable requirements and labeled with the exact places they appear. You want Section L converted into a step-by-step set of instructions with the publisher's quirks preserved: heading names, file formats, font sizes, margins, page limits, submission portals, and deadlines. You want Section M expressed as the agency's scoring playbook, with the evaluators' priorities quoted in their own words so you can write directly to what they will grade. From those ingredients you produce a single requirements matrix that maps each instruction in L to the matching task in C and the corresponding factor in M. That matrix is not decoration; it is your backbone. It becomes your outline, your QA checklist, your receipt when you claim compliance, and your shield if someone ever challenges the integrity of your bid.

Next, mirror Section L to build your outline. Do not paraphrase headings and do not improvise order. If L wants "Technical Approach" before "Management and Staffing," give it what it wants. Assign page budgets to every part of the outline and keep the cross-references to C and M right there in the margins so each sentence knows which rule it serves and which score it seeks. Now draft one small subsection at a time. Resist the urge to pour the whole ocean into the model; success is granular. Hand it your past performance blurbs, resumes, org charts, and value proposition statements. Then tell it precisely what to write: only this subsection, within a tight word range, in active voice, and with explicit brackets that show which requirement from L and which factor from M each paragraph supports. Demand at least one measurable metric for every claim. If the system tries to glide on adjectives and reputation, press it back toward numbers.

When the words are on the page, insist on evidence. Ask the model to replace soft language with hard commitments: response times in minutes, completion percentages on schedule, defect thresholds per quarter, acceptance criteria by task. Where prose gets muddy, drop in a small table that clarifies the metrics, the targets, and how you will verify each one. If a sentence cannot answer, in plain English, which requirement it fulfills or which evaluation factor it will score, cut it. Style is seasoning; compliance and proof are the meal.

Close every subsection with a compliance sweep. This is not copyediting; it is pre-award risk management. Have the model check the draft against Section L and return a punch list of missing elements, over-length risks, prohibited formatting, broken labels, orphaned claims, and references that need sources. Work the list to zero before you move on. Lock your voice before you scale your drafting. Paste in two or three pages of your brand language and instruct the model to mirror sentence length, rhythm, vocabulary, and the temperature of your tone. Enforce it with each pass so the final reads like one author, not twelve subcontractors.

You can speed the repetitive moves without cheapening the craft. Ask for an executive summary that answers four questions, in that order: Why us, Why now, Why safe, Why cost-sound. Keep it tight and end with a two-sentence close that previews your win themes. Convert resumes into role-fit pages that emphasize tasks aligned to the SOW and the evaluation criteria, preserving dates, titles, and certifications while foregrounding the outcomes that matter. Build a risk register straight from the environment described in the SOW: list the six most credible risks, estimate likelihood and impact, and state your mitigation in language a contracting officer could defend. If your approach benefits from a visual flow, have the system write the captions for a six-step operations diagram and tie at least two steps to the metrics you intend to report.

All that drafting power does not change the discipline of deciding whether to chase the work. Use AI to run a fast screen before you throw bodies at a long shot. Have it read the RFP and score your fit on a handful of practical dimensions like scope alignment, past performance similarity, staffing readiness, schedule feasibility, capital and bonding capacity, contract type risk, the evaluation method in play, small-business program advantage, geography and logistics, and the overall compliance burden and require it to explain every number in a sentence and flag any true show-stopper. If the average falls below the threshold you set, or if a single disqualifying requirement appears, do not romance the opportunity. Consider subcontracting, consider teaming, or pass. If the triage clears, ask the system for a deeper cut. It should surface incumbent clues from public records and prior awards, expose quiet must-haves that behave like mandatory requirements, and draft a one-page capture plan that lists the customer's hot buttons, your three win themes, your three discriminators, your three real risks, the proof you can put on the table, and your first contact moves. Then you, not the machine, decide whether the pursuit deserves calendar space.

Research remains a contact sport, but AI can do the running so you can do the reading. Have it assemble an agency snapshot with mission, current leadership priorities, budget trajectory, strategic plans, and a handful of similar awards from the last two years. Demand sources and dates in plain view. Ask for competitor snapshots that summarize strengths and gaps, likely price posture, teaming habits, and any performance patterns that recur across records. Use the model to frame a parametric price picture that is labor mapped to locality wages, burdens broken out in the open, fee presented with a rationale and compare that picture to values from similar awards. Wherever your number swings more than ten percent from the pattern, write the assumption that explains it in a way a contracting officer could track. Finally, let the system assemble a compliance pack so no signature gets missed and no form sinks the ship: list every affidavit, bond, certificate, and attachment, identify who signs and whether notarization is required, and translate due dates into calendar dates that match your actual submission plan.

None of this gives you license to abandon ethics or accuracy. Do not feed the machine proprietary material from partners or suppliers without permission. Do not allow it to fabricate citations, dates, certifications, references, or pricing. Treat any factual statement as suspect until a human checks it against the source document. Keep a provenance log that records what you fed the system, what it produced, who edited the result, and when the decision to use it was made. A simple spreadsheet will do. If questions ever arise, you will have receipts that show a clean, defensible process.

Two final notes belong in this chapter and in your culture. First, write to Section M, not to your ego. AI can help you find the exact phrases evaluators use to describe value; make those phrases do work in your narrative so scorers do not have to infer intent. Second, remember the metaphor that keeps you honest: you are the chef, the model is the sous-chef. Let it prep the onions at light speed, keep the stove spotless, and portion the plates precisely. You still taste the sauce, fix the seasoning, reject the dish that isn't ready, and send out the meal you stand behind. That is how you bring AI into this chapter. Firm hand on the wheel, clean trail behind you, numbers in the light, and language that sounds like you and leave the reader with something more than a promise: a method that travels, scales, and wins.

Lesson VIII

KEEP YA EAR TO THE STREETS
(Check on the Status of the Contract Award)

After submitting your bid, it's important to ensure that your contact information is accurate and up to date. This is crucial because the government agency will need to contact you if you are awarded the contract. Make sure that the email address, phone number, and mailing address you provided are correct and easily accessible.

It's also a good idea to designate a point of contact within your organization who will be responsible for receiving and responding to any communication related to the bid. This person should be easily accessible and responsive to any inquiries or requests for information from the agency.

Another important step after submitting your bid is to keep track of the timeline for the contract award. This includes knowing when the bid review period ends, when the contract will be awarded, and when work is expected to begin. This information can be found in the bid solicitation and should be added to your organization's calendar or project management system to ensure that deadlines are met.

If you are not awarded the contract, it's important to review the reasons why and identify any areas where you can improve for future bids. This can help you refine your bidding process and increase your chances of success in future opportunities.

If your bid is awarded, it's important to have a plan in place for fulfilling the contract requirements. This includes having the necessary staff and resources in place, as well as a project plan and timeline for completing the work.

After submitting a bid, the procurement agency will review the proposals and evaluate them based on the criteria outlined in the solicitation. The agency will then select the winning bidder and issue a "Notice of Intent to Award" (NOIA) to that bidder. The agency will also issue a public NOIA.

The NOIA is not a guarantee that the contract will be awarded to the bidder. It is simply a notice to inform the bidder that they have been selected as the apparent winner of the contract. The bidder must then wait for the "Notice of Award" (NOA) to be issued, which is the official document confirming that they have been awarded the contract.

During the period between the NOIA and the NOA, the procurement department will conduct a final review of the selected bidder's qualifications and past performance to ensure they meet all requirements. If any issues arise during this review, the procurement department may revoke the NOIA and select a different bidder.

If a bidder disagrees with the award decision, they may challenge it by filing a protest within a certain timeframe. This timeframe is typically a 10-day period after the NOIA has been issued. The protest process varies depending on the procurement department and the state or local laws governing the procurement process. However, in general, the protesting bidder must provide a detailed explanation of why they believe the award decision was incorrect or unfair.

The procurement department will review the protest and may hold a hearing or request additional information before making a final decision. If the protest is upheld, the agency may revoke the NOIA and select a different bidder. If the protest is denied, the original award decision will stand.

It is important to note that challenges should only be filed if there is evidence of a violation of the bidding process or other improprieties. Frivolous challenges can harm a bidder's reputation and make it more difficult to secure future contracts. It is equally important for bidders to thoroughly review the solicitation documents and understand the evaluation criteria before submitting a bid. This can help minimize the risk of an unsuccessful bid and potential protests.

Once a Notice of Intent to Award (NOIA) has been received, it is important to respond to it promptly. This is the agency's way of informing bidders that they are the preferred candidate for the contract. The NOIA typically includes details about the proposed contract, including the scope of work, pricing, and timeline.

When responding to the NOIA, it is important to carefully review all of the details and make sure that all of the information is correct. Any errors or discrepancies should be addressed immediately. This is also a good opportunity to ask any additional questions or clarify any concerns about the contract.

If the response to the NOIA is satisfactory, the agency will then issue a Notice of Award (NOA). This is the official notification that the bidder has been selected for the contract. The NOA will include the terms and conditions of the contract, as well as any other relevant information, such as the start date and duration of the contract.

Once the NOA has been received, it is important to carefully review all of the terms and conditions and ensure that they are acceptable. If there are any issues or concerns, they should be raised with the agency immediately.

It is also important to make sure that all required documentation and certifications are in order. This may include insurance certificates, bonding information, and other legal documents. Failure to provide these documents promptly can result in delays in the contract award process.

During the contract award phase, it is important to review the contract thoroughly to ensure that everything is accurate and in line with what was agreed upon during the bidding process. This is also a good time to consult with an attorney to address any changes that need to be made to the contract, a process commonly referred to as "redlining".

Redlining involves reviewing the contract and making changes or adding new provisions as needed. It is important to ensure that any changes made are mutually agreed upon by both parties and that they are fair and reasonable. This process can be time-consuming, but it is important to make sure that the contract is as accurate as possible before it is signed.

During the redlining process, it is also important to make sure that all of the terms and conditions of the contract are clearly understood. This includes the reporting requirements, billing procedures, and project particulars that may not have been included in the bid. It is important to address any questions or concerns at this stage to avoid any confusion or miscommunication down the line.

Another important aspect of reviewing the contract is to make sure that all parties involved are clear on their respective roles and responsibilities. This includes identifying a project manager within your company and a point of contact with the government agency. It is important to establish good communication between both parties to ensure that the project runs smoothly. Once the contract has been signed, it is legally binding and all parties must abide by its terms and conditions.

When working with subcontractors, it is important to establish a contract with them that clearly outlines their responsibilities and expectations. Even though the subcontractor is not required to sign the contract with the government agency, there still needs to be an agreement with the subcontractor binding them to their part of the contract. This will help ensure that everyone is on the same page and that the subcontractor understands their role in the project.

The contract should include details such as the scope of work, timeline, payment terms, and any other relevant information. By establishing a clear agreement with your subcontractor, you can help ensure that the project runs smoothly and that everyone is held accountable for their responsibilities.

A kick-off meeting is an important step in the contracting process that occurs after the contract has been awarded. This meeting brings together the government agency and the contractor to discuss the project, establish expectations, and ensure that everyone is on the same page.

During the kick-off meeting, the government agency will typically review the scope of work, project schedule, and any other relevant details. The contractor will have an opportunity to ask questions and clarify any issues. The meeting is also an opportunity for the contractor to introduce their team and discuss roles and responsibilities.

The kick-off meeting is also a good time to establish lines of communication between the contractor and the government agency. This includes identifying key contacts and setting expectations for how and when communication will occur.

Additionally, the kick-off meeting is an opportunity to establish goals and milestones for the project. The government agency will likely have specific requirements for reporting and progress updates, which should be discussed and agreed upon during the meeting.

The contractor should also take the opportunity during the kick-off meeting to ensure that they fully understand the expectations of the government agency. This includes the quality of work, safety requirements, and compliance with regulations.

Overall, the kick-off meeting is a critical step in establishing a successful partnership between the government agency and the contractor. It sets the tone for the project and helps ensure that everyone is aligned on expectations and goals.

After a contract has been awarded, a kick-off meeting is held to formally begin the project. One of the first things that should be done is to identify a project manager within your company who will be responsible for overseeing the project. The project manager will be the main point of contact with the government agency, so it is important to choose someone who is knowledgeable about the project and has good communication skills.

During the kick-off meeting, reporting requirements, billing procedures, and project particulars that may not have been included in the bid should be discussed. The project manager should take detailed notes and make sure that everyone is on the same page. This is also a good time to establish lines of communication between your company and the government agency and to ensure that everyone knows who to contact in case of any issues or concerns.

It is important to have a clear understanding of the reporting requirements for the project. The government agency may require regular progress reports, financial reports, or other types of reports. The project manager should be aware of these requirements and should ensure that they are met on time.

Billing procedures should also be discussed during the kick-off meeting. The government agency may have specific requirements for invoicing and payment. It is important to understand these requirements and to make sure that your company can meet them.

During the kick-off meeting, project particulars that may not have been included in the bid should be discussed. This could include details about the timeline for the project, specific requirements for materials or equipment, or other details that were not mentioned in the bid. It is important to address these details early on to avoid any misunderstandings later on.

After the kick-off meeting, it is important to establish a regular schedule for communication between your company and the government agency. This could include regular meetings, phone calls, or email updates. The project manager should ensure that everyone is informed of any updates or changes to the project and that any issues or concerns are addressed promptly.

If there are any issues or concerns that arise during the project, it is important to address them as soon as possible. This could involve contacting the government agency to discuss the issue or making changes to the project plan to address the concern.

For the Hood

Yo, congratulations on winning that bid, fam! Now you gotta make sure you don't drop the ball in the contract award phase. This is when you'll work out all the details with the government agency and make sure everything is on point.

First things first, make sure your contact information is correct so they can reach you when they're ready to award the contract. You don't wanna miss out on that money, my dude.

Once you get that "Notice of Intent to Award" or that "Notice of Award," you gotta act fast. Respond to that joint ASAP and get ready to kick off the project. But hold up, don't forget that 10-day challenge period after the NOIA. If you wanna contest the award, you gotta do it within those 10 days or else you're outta luck.

Now, you gotta establish a contract with your subcontractor, even though they ain't required to sign the contract with the agency. You still need to have an agreement with them to make sure they're on board with their part of the contract.

It's also time to identify a project manager within your company and a point of contact with the government agency. During this kick-off meeting, y'all gotta discuss all the project particulars that weren't in the bid, plus reporting requirements and billing procedures. Make sure you're on the same page, ya heard? And don't forget about reviewing the contract during this phase. You might need to consult with a lawyer to "redline" the contract and make any necessary changes. Better safe than sorry, my man.

Yo, when you're negotiating a contract with the government, you gotta watch your back like you're signing a 360 record deal. The government wants to make sure they're getting their money's worth, and you gotta make sure you're not getting screwed over in the process. Just like how some record labels try to take all your profits and leave you with nothing, the government can slip some sneaky stuff into the contract that can leave you with the short end of the stick. That's why it's crucial to read that contract with a fine-toothed comb and make sure you're not getting played.

Last but not least, you gotta stay on top of your game throughout the entire contract period. Make sure you're meeting all the requirements and deliverables and keep your client happy. That's how you build a good reputation and get more government contracts in the future.

So, keep grinding and handle your business, my G. The contract award phase is just the beginning of a successful project.

Lesson IX

DON'T PSYCH YASELF OUT
(Defeating Imposter Syndrome)

Imposter syndrome is a common feeling among entrepreneurs, particularly when bidding for government contracts. It's the feeling that you're not good enough or qualified enough to be doing what you're doing. The truth is, many people experience imposter syndrome when it comes to bidding on government contracts, but it doesn't have to stop you from pursuing this lucrative business opportunity.

First and foremost, it's important to recognize that you are not alone in feeling this way. Many entrepreneurs experience imposter syndrome, particularly when it comes to government contracts. However, the key is to push past these feelings and focus on your skills, expertise, and qualifications. You are a qualified and capable entrepreneur, and you have something valuable to offer the government.

One way to combat imposter syndrome is to do your research. Learn as much as you can about the government contracting process, the agency you are bidding for, and the specific project you are bidding on. The more you know, the more confident you will feel about your ability to bid on and win the contract.

Another way to combat imposter syndrome is to surround yourself with supportive and encouraging individuals. Seek mentors, peers, or colleagues who can provide guidance and support as you navigate the government contracting process. Additionally, seek out opportunities to network and connect with other entrepreneurs who are also bidding on government contracts.

It's also important to have a strong team in place to support you throughout the bidding process. This may include accountants, legal professionals, and other experts who can provide guidance and support as needed. By having a strong team in place, you can feel more confident and prepared as you move forward in the bidding process.

Another important factor is to develop a strong value proposition that showcases your unique skills and expertise. This can help differentiate you from other bidders and make your proposal stand out. Be sure to highlight any experience or qualifications that make you uniquely qualified for the project.

In addition, it's important to be organized and stay on top of deadlines. This means keeping track of important dates, completing all necessary paperwork, and submitting your bid on time. By staying organized and on top of things, you can feel more in control and confident throughout the process.

If you do experience imposter syndrome during the bidding process, it's important to remember that these feelings are normal and common. However, it's important to not let these feelings hold you back from pursuing this lucrative business opportunity. Take the time to reflect on your skills and qualifications, surround yourself with supportive individuals, and stay organized and focused throughout the process.

One of the biggest contributors to imposter syndrome is the negative influences around you. People who doubt you or tell you that you can't do something can intensify these feelings and make it difficult to move forward.

If you have people in your life who are not supportive of your business aspirations, it may be time to re-evaluate those relationships. Surround yourself with positive influences, people who believe in you and your capabilities. Having a strong support system can make all the difference when it comes to overcoming imposter syndrome. It's important to surround yourself with people who believe in you and your abilities, and who will encourage and support you along the way. This can be family members, friends, colleagues, or even other vendors in the industry.

Another way to combat imposter syndrome is to focus on your strengths and accomplishments. Keep a record of your successes and celebrate your achievements along the way. This will help you build your confidence and remind you of your capabilities. It's important to remember that everyone has strengths and weaknesses and that it's okay to ask for help when you need it.

It is also important to remember that even the largest multinational companies started small, and with hard work and perseverance, they were able to grow and succeed in the government contracting space. Examples of these companies include Lockheed Martin, General Dynamics, and Boeing.

Don't let imposter syndrome hold you back from achieving your goals in government contracting. Take the necessary steps to build your confidence, skills, and knowledge, and remember that every successful company started somewhere. With dedication and hard work, you can achieve success in this field.

For the Hood

Let's talk about impostor syndrome. This is that feeling where you doubt yourself like you don't belong. It's when you think you're a fraud and that everyone is going to find out. It's like you're playing a role, but you don't feel like it's really you.

Impostor syndrome can be especially tough when you're trying to bid on government contracts. You might think, "Who am I to do this? I'm not good enough." But let me tell you, you are good enough. You got this. You just need to believe in yourself.

One of the biggest reasons people struggle with impostor syndrome is because they compare themselves to others. They think everyone else has it all figured out and they don't. But the truth is, everyone has their own struggles and challenges. Don't compare yourself to others, focus on your own journey.

Another thing that can contribute to impostor syndrome is negative self-talk. You need to be your own biggest supporter, not your own worst critic. When you hear that negative voice in your head, shut it down. Replace it with positive affirmations and focus on your strengths.

It's also important to surround yourself with people who believe in you and support your goals. You don't need anyone around you who is going to bring you down or make you doubt yourself. To hell with the haters. Find your tribe, people who inspire you and lift you up.

Remember, even the biggest companies started somewhere. Jigga didn't wake up with a billion dollars, and the Roc didn't start as a mega-label. Look at the success stories of other businesses in the government contracting space. They all started with a dream and the determination to make it happen. You can do the same.

Impostor syndrome is tough, but it doesn't have to hold you back. Believe in yourself, focus on your journey, and surround yourself with positive people. You got this.

Lesson X

BUY THE BLACK CARD
(Minority Business Certifications)

Minority-owned businesses are playing an increasingly important role in the economy, and obtaining minority business certifications can help these businesses gain access to government contracts and other opportunities that may be otherwise difficult to secure. If you are a minority business owner, it's important to understand the certification process and the benefits that come with being certified.

Firstly, what is a minority-owned business? In the United States, a minority-owned business is one that is at least 51% owned, operated, and controlled by one or more individuals who are members of a minority group. These groups include African Americans, Hispanic Americans, Native Americans, Asian Americans, Pacific Islanders, and women.

Obtaining minority business certifications can provide many benefits, including access to government contracts, access to grants, and loans, and access to networking opportunities with other minority-owned businesses. Certification can also help to boost your business's reputation, as many organizations seek out and prefer to do business with certified minority-owned businesses.

Several organizations offer minority business certifications, including the National Minority Supplier Development Council (NMSDC), the Women's

Business Enterprise National Council (WBENC), and the Small Business Administration's 8(a) Business Development Program.

The 8(a) certification is a program designed by the Small Business Administration (SBA) to assist socially and economically disadvantaged individuals in starting, growing, and developing their businesses. To qualify for the program, an individual must be a member of a socially and economically disadvantaged group, such as African Americans, Hispanics, Native Americans, Asian Pacific Americans, and Subcontinent Asian Americans, among others. Additionally, the individual must demonstrate a potential for success and have a personal net worth that does not exceed $250,000, among other eligibility criteria.

The 8(a) program provides a range of benefits to certified businesses, including sole-source contracts of up to $4 million for goods and services and up to $6.5 million for manufacturing. The program also provides business development assistance, such as training, counseling, and access to government surplus property and excess inventory. Moreover, the program offers a mentor-protégé program, which pairs 8(a) firms with larger, established companies to provide guidance, support, and access to opportunities.

To apply for the 8(a) certification, an individual must submit an application through the SBA. The application process involves a review of the individual's personal and business financial statements, tax returns, and other documentation, as well as an interview with an SBA representative. Once certified, the individual must submit annual updates and demonstrate progress toward their business development goals.

The 8(a) certification can be a valuable tool for minority-owned businesses looking to gain access to government contracts and business development resources. However, it is important to note that the application process can be lengthy and requires a significant amount of documentation and preparation. Additionally, the program has a nine-year limit, after which businesses must transition out of the program and compete in the open market.

The 8(a) certification process comes with several benefits that can help give minority businesses a leg up in the federal contracting arena. However, it is important to note that there is one potential drawback to the 8(a) program. When competing for 8(a) sole source contracts, all of the competitors are required to be 8(a) certified. This means that the playing field is even and your business is competing against other businesses that have also received the 8(a) certification.

In contrast, in the open market, there is often a clear advantage for certified minority businesses as they are competing with non-minority businesses. However, in the 8(a) program, all of the competitors have received the same certification, so the advantage is not as clear. Nonetheless, this does not mean that the 8(a) program is not worth pursuing. The program still provides many benefits such as access to set-aside contracts, mentorship opportunities, and assistance with business development. It is up to each business owner to weigh the pros and cons and determine if the 8(a) program is the right fit for their business.

To be eligible for certification, your business must meet certain criteria, such as being at least 51% owned by members of a minority group, being managed and controlled by members of a minority group, and being a for-profit business that is headquartered in the United States. The certification process can be lengthy and may require significant documentation, such as tax returns, financial statements, and proof of ownership. However, the benefits of certification can be well worth the effort.

In addition to government contracts, certification can also provide access to corporate supplier diversity programs, which many large companies have in place to ensure that a certain percentage of their suppliers are minority-owned businesses. This can be a valuable source of business for minority-owned companies, as these programs often involve long-term contracts and stable revenue streams.

It's important to note that obtaining minority business certifications does not guarantee business or success, but it can certainly increase your chances of success. Once certified, it's important to continue to network and market your business effectively to take full advantage of the opportunities that certification can provide.

The DBE certification, offered by the Department of Transportation, is a valuable certification to have for minority-owned businesses. The best part? The application is free! One unique benefit of the DBE certification is that the certifying agency will send your information to the certifying agency for the MBE for consideration. This provides an opportunity to potentially get your MBE for free.

It's important to note that although the DBE certification is issued by the DOT, it is not limited to being used solely on transportation contracts. Many local municipalities and other organizations also accept this certification for various contract opportunities. This certification can provide a significant advantage in securing contracts and increasing the visibility of your business.

However, it's important to note that the DBE certification process can be rigorous and time-consuming. It requires a significant amount of documentation and proof of eligibility, and the certification process can take several months. It's essential to carefully review the requirements and ensure that your business meets the criteria before beginning the application process.

Once certified, it's important to maintain your certification by regularly submitting the required documentation and participating in the necessary training programs. The certification is typically valid for a set period, and it's crucial to stay on top of the renewal process to avoid any lapses in certification.

The ByBlack Certification is the newest addition to minority business certifications, but it's one that's making waves in the black community. This certification is issued through the U.S. Black Chamber of Commerce, and it's the only certification that requires you to be African American. That's right, you can't just be any minority - you have to be black.

But why is this certification so important? Well, for one, it's specifically designed to help black-owned businesses gain access to government contracts and other opportunities. It's no secret that black-owned businesses face unique challenges when it comes to competing in the marketplace. ByBlack

Certification is aimed at leveling the playing field and giving these businesses a fair shot.

Another reason the ByBlack Certification is so valuable is that it provides networking opportunities with other black-owned businesses. It can be difficult for minority-owned businesses to connect with one another and build relationships, but the ByBlack Certification makes it easier. When you're part of the ByBlack network, you have access to a community of other black-owned businesses that are all working toward the same goals.

The ByBlack Certification process isn't easy - it requires a lot of documentation and proof of ownership. But the effort is worth it, especially for businesses that are struggling to get a foothold in their respective industries. In addition to the certification itself, the U.S. Black Chamber of Commerce offers a range of resources and support services to certified businesses.

Of course, the ByBlack Certification isn't the only minority business certification out there. Many other certifications are available to businesses owned by minorities, women, veterans, and other underrepresented groups. These certifications can also provide access to government contracts, networking opportunities, and other valuable resources.

When deciding which certification is right for your business, it's important to do your research and understand the requirements and benefits of each. Some certifications may be more appropriate for your business than others, depending on your industry, location, and other factors.

Ultimately, the goal of minority business certifications is to create a more equitable and diverse marketplace. By taking advantage of these opportunities, minority-owned businesses can gain the resources and support they need to succeed and thrive. The ByBlack Certification is just one example of how organizations are working to support black-owned businesses and promote economic empowerment in the black community.

Going after multiple minority certifications can be a smart move for businesses looking to increase their chances of winning government contracts. Each certification may have its own set of fees, but the benefits of obtaining them can be significant.

For instance, the National Minority Supplier Development Council (NMSDC) charges an application fee ranging from $350 to $1,000 depending on the company's size, and an annual fee of $1,500 for certification renewal. In exchange, businesses receive access to corporate purchasing agents, networking opportunities, and other resources that can help grow their business.

Similarly, the Women's Business Enterprise National Council (WBENC) charges an application fee of $350, with annual certification fees ranging from $350 to $1,200 depending on the company's size. In addition to gaining access to corporate purchasing agents, businesses can also attend networking events, training workshops, and mentoring programs.

The fees associated with these certifications may seem steep, but the benefits they offer can be invaluable. For example, a certified minority-owned business may be more likely to win a government contract, as many agencies have quotas or goals for contracting with minority-owned businesses. Additionally, certification can help businesses stand out from their competitors and enhance their reputation.

By obtaining multiple certifications, businesses can increase their chances of winning contracts and accessing new opportunities. For example, a business that is certified by both the NMSDC and WBENC can take advantage of both organizations' resources and connections. This can be particularly valuable for businesses looking to expand into new markets or industries.

Getting certified as a minority-owned business comes with many advantages, one of which is the increased visibility of potential contracting opportunities. When certified, your business is added to a database of certified minority-owned businesses that large companies actively search for. This puts you in a prime position to be considered for potential contracting and subcontracting opportunities.

By being listed in the database, it also means that companies are more likely to find you and reach out to you with opportunities that you may not have even considered. This is a great way to expand your business and gain new clients.

Furthermore, being listed in the database means that you are already pre-screened and pre-approved by the certifying agency, which can give companies the confidence to work with you. It also means that you have a leg up on your competition, as many companies are actively seeking out minority-owned businesses for contracting opportunities.

Overall, the increased visibility and exposure that comes with being certified as a minority-owned business is a huge benefit. It can lead to new opportunities and partnerships, and help to grow your business in ways that may not have been possible before.

For the Hood

Yo! You want to get ahead in the game and start getting those big government contracts? Then you need to get certified, homie. Having a minority business certification can give you a leg up in the game and open doors to big opportunities. So, let's dive into it.

One of the newest certifications out there is the ByBlack certification. It's issued through the U.S. Black Chamber of Commerce and it's only for African American businesses. Ya heard? This is a new opportunity for us to make moves in the game and get recognized for our hustle.

Now, if you're serious about getting certified, you gotta go after multiple minority certifications. Yeah, it costs some money, but trust me, it's worth it. Having multiple certifications means more opportunities, more exposure, and more chances to make those connections that can help you get to the next level.

One of the certifications you should check out is the DBE certification. And guess what, homie? It's free! This certification is offered through the Department of Transportation, and it's not just limited to transportation contracts. Local municipalities accept it too, so don't sleep on it.

The 8(a) certification is another one you should consider. It's issued by the Small Business Administration and it's specifically for businesses owned by socially and economically disadvantaged individuals. The one con is that when competing for 8(a) sole source contracts, all of the competitors are 8(a) certified. But still, having this certification can give you a boost in the game.

The best part of all of these certifications is that you'll be added to a database that big companies scour for contracting and subcontracting opportunities. They'll start reaching out to you, my friend. And that's when you know you've made it.

But hold up, one thing you gotta remember is that getting certified doesn't mean you can just sit back and wait for the opportunities to come to you. You gotta keep hustlin', keep grinding, and keep making those connections. You gotta network and let people know who you are and what you can do.

So, don't be scared to get certified, homie. It's a step in the right direction and can lead to big things for your business. Keep hustlin' and stay on your grind.

And when you get that certification, don't be afraid to show it off. Put it on your website, your business cards, and your LinkedIn profile. Let the world know that you're certified and you're proud of it.

So, if you're serious about taking your business to the next level, go ahead and get certified. Get yourself that Black Card and watch the doors of opportunity open up. You got this!

Resources

SAM.gov - This is the System for Award Management, which is the primary database for vendors and contractors who want to do business with the federal government. It allows you to register as a contractor and provides access to federal procurement opportunities.

FedBizOpps.gov - This is the Federal Business Opportunities website, which lists all open procurement opportunities for the federal government. Vendors can search for opportunities, receive updates, and submit bids and proposals.

SBA.gov - The Small Business Administration website provides resources and information for small businesses, including contracting opportunities and certification programs.

GSA.gov - The General Services Administration website is the federal government's primary procurement agency, responsible for managing government assets and contracts. The site provides access to procurement opportunities and resources for vendors.

NIGP.org - The National Institute of Government Procurement is a professional association for procurement professionals. The site provides resources and training for government procurement, including certification programs.

DLA.mil - The Defense Logistics Agency website provides information and resources for businesses interested in contracting with the Department of Defense.

USA.gov - The official website of the United States government provides information and resources for businesses interested in contracting with the government at all levels.

PTAC.gov - The Procurement Technical Assistance Center website provides training and resources for businesses interested in government contracting at the state and local levels.

NAICS.com - The North American Industry Classification System website provides a standardized system for classifying businesses and industries for contracting purposes.

GAO.gov - The Government Accountability Office website provides oversight and audit services for government agencies, including procurement activities. The site provides reports and resources for vendors and contractors.

SBA.gov - The SBA provides resources and information on various certifications for small and minority-owned businesses.

MBDA.gov - The MBDA is a federal agency that helps minority-owned businesses with a variety of resources, including certification.

NMSDC.org - The NMSDC is a private organization that provides certification for minority-owned businesses looking to work with corporate America.

WBENC.org - The WBENC provides certification for women-owned businesses seeking to work with corporations and government agencies.

NVBDC.org - The NVBDC provides certification for veteran-owned businesses looking to work with corporations and government agencies.

ByBlack.us - The ByBlack Certification is issued through the U.S. Black Chamber of Commerce and is the only certification that requires businesses to be African-American owned.

TRANSPORTATION.gov - The DBE certification is offered through the Department of Transportation and is designed to help disadvantaged businesses compete for transportation contracts.

Glossary

Procurement - the process of acquiring goods or services on behalf of an organization or government agency.

RFP (Request for Proposal) - a document that outlines the requirements and specifications of a project, and solicits bids from potential vendors.

RFQ (Request for Quote) - a document that requests a quote or bid for a specific product or service.

IFB (Invitation for Bid) - a solicitation document used to request bids from suppliers or contractors.

Bid - a proposal submitted by a supplier or contractor in response to an RFP or RFQ.

Contract - a legally binding agreement between two or more parties that outlines the terms and conditions of a business transaction.

Sole Source - a contract awarded without competition, typically for goods or services that are unique or proprietary.

Subcontractor - a company or individual that is hired by a prime contractor to perform a specific task or provide a specific service on a larger project.

Prime Contractor - the main contractor on a project who is responsible for managing and coordinating all aspects of the project.

LPTA (Lowest Price Technically Acceptable) - a type of procurement process in which the award is based solely on the lowest price that meets the technical requirements of the RFP.

Best Value - a type of procurement process in which the award is based on a combination of factors, including price, quality, and other considerations.

Performance Bond - a type of surety bond that guarantees a contractor will complete a project according to the terms and conditions of the contract.

Payment Bond - a type of surety bond that guarantees a contractor will pay all subcontractors and suppliers involved in a project.

Notice to Proceed - a document that authorizes a contractor to begin work on a project.

Change Order - a written agreement between the parties to modify the terms of an existing contract.

Invoice - a document submitted by a contractor or supplier that requests payment for goods or services rendered.

Scope of Work - a document that outlines the specific tasks or deliverables that a contractor is responsible for completing.

Technical Proposal - a detailed proposal that outlines a contractor's technical approach to a project and how they plan to meet the requirements of the RFP.

Cost Proposal - a detailed proposal that outlines a contractor's estimated costs for completing a project.

NIGP (National Institute of Governmental Purchasing) - a professional association that provides education and certification for procurement professionals.

Performance Period - The period in which the work is to be completed.

Deliverables - The tangible or intangible items that the contractor is responsible for providing under the contract.

Contract Price - The amount that the government will pay the contractor for their services.

Payment Terms - The specific terms and schedule for payment of the contract price.

Indemnification - The requirement for the contractor to compensate the government for any losses, damages, or liability arising out of the contract.

Warranty - The contractor's guarantee that their work will meet the agreed-upon specifications and standards.

Termination for Convenience - The government's right to terminate the contract for any reason, without cause, with proper notice.

Termination for Default - The government's right to terminate the contract for cause, such as failure to perform or breach of contract.

Force Majeure - A clause that excuses the parties from performance under the contract due to unforeseeable circumstances beyond their control, such as natural disasters or war.

Intellectual Property - The ownership and rights associated with any intellectual property created or used in the performance of the contract.

Subcontracting - The ability for the contractor to hire subcontractors to perform some or all of the work under the contract.

Non-Disclosure Agreement - A legal agreement that prohibits the contractor from disclosing confidential or proprietary information of the government or other parties involved in the contract.

Conflict of Interest - A clause that requires the contractor to disclose any potential conflicts of interest that may arise during the performance of the contract.

Dispute Resolution - The procedures and methods for resolving any disputes that may arise between the parties during the performance of the contract.

www.ingramcontent.com/pod-product-compliance
Lightning Source LLC
Chambersburg PA
CBHW061417300426
44114CB00015B/1965